HOW TO SUR

HOW TO SURVIVE
THE LOSS OF
A PARENT

A Guide for Adults

LOIS F. AKNER, C.S.W.,
WITH CATHERINE WHITNEY

QUILL • WILLIAM MORROW • NEW YORK

Library of Congress Cataloging-in-Publication Data
Akner, Lois F.
How to survive the loss of a parent : a guide for adults / by Lois F. Akner with Catherine Whitney.
p.   cm.
Includes bibliographical references.
ISBN 0-688-13791-1
1. Bereavement-Psychological aspects.   2. Parents—Death—Psychological aspects.   3. Adult children—Psychology.   4. Grief.   I. Whitney, Catherine.
II. Title.
BF575.G7A46 1993
155.9'37-dc20   92-46213
                                                      CIP

Printed in the United States of America

First Quill Edition

6   7   8   9   10

BOOK DESIGN BY DEBBIE GLASSERMAN

To my mother and father

A PERSONAL NOTE

*Writing music is easy.
What's hard is knowing
which notes to use and
which to let fall to the
ground.*
   —Johannes Brahms

No one who knows me well is surprised that I am working in the world of death. In fact, one of my dear friends, Ken Lerer, who originally discussed the idea of this book with me, suggested that maybe I'd become the "Dr. Ruth of Death"—in the sense of bringing a subject that makes so many people uncomfortable out of the closet. Ken's comment made me laugh, but it also touched on the reason why my work and this book are so important. Sex has been out of the closet for a long time, but we're still squeamish about discussing death. When I tell people about this book, their first reaction is often, "A book about what?"

As I look back on how I came to do this work, it all seems fitting that I would choose this path, given the circumstances of my own family—or at least, my perception of them. (As you will learn when you read this book, different family members often reach varying conclusions about the meaning of things.)

For a very long time, I believed that the only major thing that ever happened in our family was my father's death. It influenced what I did; it excused what I couldn't do. Everything else seemed to be viewed through the lens of that event. Unlike the people who come to my group, whose parents died when they were adults, I was only six years old when my father died. His illness left him lying for nine months in a hospital bed set up in our dining room. I was, of course, too young to fully understand what was happening, but I recall that my family's response was to go on and try to be "normal." In those days, death was deeply in the closet, and hanging alongside it was Cancer (with a big C), the cause of my father's death. An example of the extent to which this was unmentionable is the fact that my mother, who is one of six siblings, did not discuss the nature of my father's illness or the potential fatality of it with any of them. Although it eventually became obvious that he was very ill and probably dying, it was never stated openly.

I have since learned about some of the work involved in keeping my father's illness a secret. For example, his own mother was never told her son was sick and dying. Who knows what she thought when he stopped visiting her! When my father was in the hospital, his sister would visit him there; on at least a couple of occasions, she had their mother in the car with her. I am told she would park the car near the hospital, tell her mother she had to do an errand or visit a sick "friend," and then run in to visit her brother while their mother, assumed to be oblivious, waited in the car.

My father's mother died six months before he did, still

having never been told of her son's illness. We will never know what she figured out on her own. She never said.

The desperate drive for normalcy, the secrecy about cancer and death, and the desire to "protect" everyone, including my father, took a toll on all of us: my mother, who couldn't share her worry and concern; my father, who pretended that he believed he was going to get better; my aunt, who, having visited her brother in the hospital, then had to return to the car and pretend to her mother that she had just done an errand; and, of course, on me and my older brother, who were never given a chance to ask questions or talk about our fears.

Admittedly, in those days there were few places we could go for advice about handling illness and death. No one knew what to do, and there was no one to ask—at least no one who seemed to know better. Looking back, it would have been useful for us to give voice to our feelings, express our confusion, ask questions, and acknowledge the inevitability of the loss. Like so many families, mine tried to normalize quickly, even though that was impossible. The three survivors (my mother, my brother, and I) never really told one another what was in our hearts. The script was written: We would continue to protect one another and ourselves. Over time, the script became encased in cement, until it seemed impenetrable.

When I finally began, after many years, to chip away at the cement so I could see what was underneath, it was very hard and took a long time. In seeking the truth, my premise was that if something begins with a falsehood or distortion, everything that follows is off center and unsteady. That's why family secrets cause so much harm; they leave out information without which other things never really make sense. So, long before I ever came to do this work, I knew I had to open some of my own doors if I had any hope of gaining freedom from the constrictions of the past. That task included being able to assess my own role in creating the system in which my family operated. A significant part of my evolution was to learn to see everyone in the family, dead or alive, to the best of my ability, respect them for who they are and were, and not hold them endlessly responsible for not being different.

At first my impetus for learning didn't seem to have anything to do with my father's death. But as I began to dig, I found it at the root of my search. Actually, that is not uncommon. One researcher states that one third of all those who seek therapy have had difficulties mourning a loss, often one suffered a long time in the past. In my case, as in others, it was not the loss that brought me to treatment. But I soon saw that my work could not be complete until the old connections were rewired.

So it was that my personal journey brought me to my work as a family therapist. Some of that work took place at the 92nd Street Y in New York City, a unique organization whose mission in part is to offer ways for people to cope with the stress of life's transitions. After observing her husband's response to his father's death, a colleague of mine suggested a course for adults whose parents had died. Seven years ago, I began the course, "Losing a Parent Is Hard at Any Age."

From the beginning, I have felt as though I am being given a precious gift with each group. People share their ideas, disappointments, horrors, memories, and secrets. Quite often, they disclose to the group private things that they have never shared with anyone else. I have tremendous respect for the power of their family relationships and the authenticity of their search. My role is not to tell them what to do or how to "cure" their grief, but to offer them possibilities and a tour through the pages of their family scripts. I tell them they can choose to look in corners, open doors, peer inside, walk around, or get out their hiking boots and explore. I am constantly impressed with how willing most of them are to do the work, even when it is very painful.

I have a conviction, born of my own journey and what I have witnessed in the lives of others, that what I do is as much about family stories as it is about the specific experience of losing a parent. The two are inextricably linked. The loss of a parent represents not only the permanent removal of that person from our lives, but all the situations in the future that would have been different had he or she remained alive. The loss of a parent also brings to the forefront the complicated puzzle of relationships, past and present.

It takes courage to look inside, and often there are more questions than answers. But my own life has taught me that the exploration can lead to a fuller, happier future. Even the great tragedy of a parent's death can be a transforming experience.

ACKNOWLEDGMENTS

I could not have written this book without the help and support of many people. I especially want to thank my editor at William Morrow, Paul Bresnick, for his belief in me; my agent, Jane Dystel, for all her good advice and kindness; and my collaborator, Catherine Whitney, for making my words and ideas resonate.

I am very grateful to my good friends and colleagues who have supported me: Marlaine Walsh Selip, who thinks her friends can do anything, and without whom this book would still be an idea; Dr. Roselle Kurland, who encouraged me to start my group and to have faith in it. She has been a mentor, colleague, and friend. Dr. Barbara Stimmel has been a trusted and valued guide. I am also grateful to Christopher Shanky, Estelle Rosen, Ken Lerer, and to the staff at the 92nd Street Y.

I am thankful to my extended family who allowed me to ask questions over and over until I got them right, to my nieces, Tracy, Stephanie (who believes in this work), and Marisa; and in fond memory of Michael and Seth Klein.

Thanks, too, to the friends who have kept me steady, and to the colleagues who have supported my work. I would like to add my thanks to the people in my profession I have never met but without whom my work couldn't be done. As in families, they have passed on a legacy.

Finally, I want to express my deepest appreciation to the many people who have shared their thoughts, feelings, memories, and experiences in my group. I hope they know that their contribution has been great to me professionally and to others who will benefit by hearing their stories.

CONTENTS

THE GROUP

Following are the men and women whom you will meet in this book. Each one is struggling, as you may be, with the death of a parent or both parents.

NAME: Amanda
AGE: Fifty
MARITAL STATUS: Single
SIBLINGS: Brother, forty-six
PARENT'S DEATH: Mother, seventy-four, died from a heart attack six months ago; father, eighty, still living.

NAME: Irene
AGE: Sixty-eight
MARITAL STATUS: Widowed ten years; daughter, forty-two, lives in California
SIBLINGS: Brother, sixty-two

PARENTS' DEATHS: Father, ninety-two, died one year ago; mother died twenty years ago at age sixty-eight.

NAME: Jane
AGE: Forty-two
MARITAL STATUS: Single
SIBLINGS: Only child
PARENTS' DEATHS: Mother, sixty-five, who had asthma, died of Adrenalin overdose—possibly suicide—one year ago; father, sixty-seven, died of prostate cancer seven months ago.

NAME: Matt
AGE: Thirty-six
MARITAL STATUS: Single
SIBLINGS: Brother, forty
PARENTS' DEATHS: Mother, seventy-nine, died of heart disease four months ago; father died twenty-six years ago in an industrial accident.

NAME: Arlene
AGE: Thirty-seven
MARITAL STATUS: Engaged to be married
SIBLINGS: Brother, thirty-two
PARENT'S DEATH: Father, eighty, died of a heart attack eight months ago; mother, seventy-five, still living. Parents were divorced.

NAME: Mary Ann
AGE: Forty-five

MARITAL STATUS: Married; son, twenty-two; daughter, nineteen

SIBLINGS: Brother, fifty; brother, forty-seven; sister thirty-nine

PARENTS' DEATHS: Mother, seventy-two, died of angina four months ago; father died ten years ago of cancer when he was sixty-four.

NAME: Patricia
AGE: Thirty-four
MARITAL STATUS: Divorced; son, five
SIBLINGS: Sister, thirty-eight; sister, twenty-nine
PARENT'S DEATH: Father, seventy-two, who was a Holocaust survivor, died six months ago of a heart attack; mother, sixty-four, still living.

NAME: Eileen
AGE: Thirty-five
MARITAL STATUS: Married, no children
SIBLINGS: Brother, forty; sister, thirty-eight
PARENTS' DEATHS: Mother, seventy, died of breast cancer six months ago; father, seventy, died of liver disease—the effects of alcoholism—about three years ago.

NAME: Richard
AGE: Twenty-eight
MARITAL STATUS: Married; daughter, six months
SIBLINGS: Brother, thirty-three
PARENT'S DEATH: Father, sixty-three, died of a stroke eight months ago; mother, sixty, lives with him.

NAME: Helen
AGE: Forty
MARITAL STATUS: Married; daughter, two
SIBLINGS: Brother, died in childhood
PARENTS' DEATHS: Father, sixty-seven, died two years ago of heart failure; mother died of cancer twenty-four years ago.

NAME: Barry
AGE: Thirty-four
MARITAL STATUS: Single
SIBLINGS: Sister, forty-nine; sister, forty-six
PARENT'S DEATH: Father, sixty-four, died five months ago from a twenty-year battle with melanoma; mother, sixty-one, still living.

NAME: Marian
AGE: Twenty-three
MARITAL STATUS: Single
SIBLINGS: Brother, thirty-five
PARENT'S DEATH: Mother, fifty-seven, died three months ago in an accident; father, fifty-eight, still alive. Parents were divorced and father is remarried.

Author's Note: The names, descriptions, and many of the identifying circumstances of the people in this group have been altered to protect their privacy. In some cases, individuals represent composites of people who have attended my workshop over the years.

HOW TO SURVIVE THE LOSS OF A PARENT

_____ ▬▬▬ _____

CHAPTER ONE

ENTERING THE WORLD
OF MOURNING

Everyone can master a grief but he that has it.
—William Shakespeare

On a cool evening in late September, I leave my office and walk twelve blocks to the community center where I am beginning a new series of workshops for adults who have lost a parent.

I have been doing this series three times a year for the past seven years, and you'd think I'd be used to it by now. But every new beginning makes me feel humbled. The people who come to these groups are experiencing real agony because a parent has died. They are in mourning, and the experience has knocked all the wind out of their sails. Their grief is often all-consuming. As one woman put it, most graphically, "Every day of my life I look down a long, dark tunnel and see no glimmer of light." They've come to me, to this group, because they can't find a way to recover on their own. Friends, spouses, siblings, surviving parents—all the people who might have been so supportive at the beginning—have moved beyond the point of patience and are saying, "Enough already. Get on with your life." But their bereavement is tangible and unshakable, and they just can't.

If you're reading this book, you (or someone you care about) may be feeling the same overwhelming sadness, and you don't know what to do or where to turn. You may be having trouble understanding the hold this grief has over your life. Maybe you fear you are way out of bounds and nobody else could possibly react this way. Depending on the relationship you had with your parent, you may even think your reaction is inexplicable. You, too, may be finding that everyone around you has lost patience and doesn't want to listen anymore or look at your sad face.

If this is your reality, I invite you to join the journey of a particular group of people who share a similar experience. In the pages of this book, I will introduce you to twelve men and women who are struggling to cope with the loss of a parent or both parents. They are ordinary people having what for them is an extraordinary experience.

As I prepare to meet with the group and contemplate what I will say to them, I am aware that every one of the twelve people who walks into the room this evening will think I know more than they do about life. What they hope is that I can wave a magic wand and make it all better. They often like to get a guarantee before they sign up. Almost inevitably they ask, "Will this group help me?" My answer is not always the one they're looking for: "Not necessarily. Sometimes you need to let yourself feel bad at the beginning. After all, we kick up a lot of strong emotions here. You just need to know you can survive those feelings." I can't promise I'll meet every one of their expectations.

Mostly they don't know what their expectations are. What I can do is give them an hour and a half a week for six consecutive weeks—set aside from all outside distractions—when they can think and talk about their parents and what they're feeling. During that time, I will open some doors and ask them to look inside, and that won't always be comfortable.

Many of the people who come to my group want to believe the relationship they had with their parents was simple and pure—the one safe haven in a hostile world. They feel abandoned and neglected when a parent dies. In their minds, this was the only relationship where they knew they had absolute, unconditional love. Their faces become pinched and fearful when they ask, "Who will ever love me the same way again?" These strong, usually competent adults, many with families of their own, are terrified because they have lost Mom or Dad or both. They are suddenly uprooted from a security so profoundly essential that they describe themselves as adult orphans. I have seen people grow fearful of love because they anticipate the pain of loss. The mother of a three-year-old daughter once said, with tremendous anguish, "How can I let her love me knowing that some day she may feel the same pain when I die?" This woman's wounds were particularly deep, but her comment illustrates just how severe the hurt and fear can be.

Others come because they feel just the opposite. Their relationship with their parents was difficult, and they never seemed to get what they wanted or needed. Now they're angry or disappointed, because things were never set right.

How to help them? Six weeks is not much time to heal these wounds. Indeed, that's not even my ultimate goal. I help them most by allowing them to have this time to grieve and by encouraging them to think about the implications of these important relationships.

What I do in the group is not therapy, although some of my group members are in therapy or decide to enter it after the workshop is completed. It is important to understand the distinction between therapy and a support group. I don't pretend that in six weeks, over a period of about nine hours, all the deep and complex issues will be resolved. For many, the group is only a first step, albeit an important one. Although the sessions are intense and frequently very revealing, people don't leave at the end with everything cleared up. Support helps people through the process of grief. Therapy helps remove any obstacles that are in the way.

Now, I think about the people in my new group. I have already had initial interviews with each of them. During the interviews, I have been touched, as I always am, by their sadness, pain, confusion—and their honest desire to get better. Sometimes their pain isn't even noticeable until they begin to speak of the parent who has died. With rare exceptions, if you came across them on the street or met them at a party, you'd never guess they were carrying such heavy burdens. But in the privacy and safety of my office, they reveal their suffering, resentment, uncertainty, and regret with remarkable candor. They seem interested in getting right down to it, in laying all their cards on the table so no time is wasted. I listen intently as they speak, and I try to say very little, for, although there is always the temptation to give advice, I know the first step is to try to hear what is said and intuit what is left unsaid.

These initial interviews are like broad strokes of a brush. I still don't feel that I know very much about these twelve people. As we continue to examine their experiences together, the portraits will acquire form and depth. Now, as I prepare to meet them as a group, I can see each person in my mind's eye—remembering what each said to me and my first impressions.

Amanda is fifty years old, a tall blonde with bright blue eyes who maintains herself in a well-kept, expensive style. She favors large, striking jewelry, which she carries with ease, and attractive tailored suits. She runs her own public relations business, and looks the part. But her self-assurance disappears when she talks about her seventy-four-year-old mother's sudden death from a heart attack six months ago. Amanda wasn't there—her father discovered her mother's body on the bathroom floor and called her, panic-stricken. She called the police before driving over herself. Her younger brother, Eric, couldn't be reached until later that evening, so Amanda took over the task of handling the ambulance service, the coroner, and the funeral home.

Now she tells me, "It seems to be taking me an exceptionally long time to get over my mother's death. It was so sudden. I wasn't ready for it." She admits that her feelings of shock and loss are tangled up with regret over the loose ends that remained in her relationship with her mother.

"I never felt my mother was satisfied with me, even though I've been quite successful in my business. I guess I wanted more time to show her I could please her."

"What do you think displeased her?"

Amanda smiles wryly. "That's easy. I never married, although I came close once or twice. My brother Eric, who is four years younger than me, has a wife and three beautiful children. In my mother's eyes, that was true success. She couldn't get over the fact that I wasn't married with a family, too. It hurt me that she felt that way, because I would have liked more than anything to be married. I just never met the right man. I'm still looking. Meanwhile, I have always made myself available to my parents and did things for them that my brother didn't have time to do."

"Are you bitter about that?"

She expresses surprise. "No, how can I be? I think my parents had a right to expect things from me, since I was their only daughter and I didn't have a family of my own. Now, with my mother gone, it's very clear that I have an obligation to my father which is greater than any of my personal needs. He is so lost without Mother. He's eighty, and they were married almost fifty-five years. He can barely take care of himself. Eric's not much help, so it's up to me. I call him every night at nine o'clock sharp. If I don't call, he gets very nervous."

"What do you talk about?" I ask curiously.

"Oh, let me see." She counts the list off on her fingers. "He tells me everything he ate that day." She mimics his tone: " 'Cereal, toast, a little margarine, tuna fish on rye with mayonnaise—no, diet spread—one pickle . . . ' " Her recitation is comical and we both laugh. "You get the picture. Then he tells me what happened—like if he had a doctor's appointment or played cards with his buddies or whatever. Then we talk about the weekend—he spends every weekend with me, so we go over the plans."

"He spends every weekend with you?"

"Yes, of course. What else is he supposed to do? He's all alone."

"How often does he spend weekends with your brother and his family?"

She shrugs. "Oh, every once in a while. But the kids

bother him. Two are teenagers and you know how they can be. The youngest is eight, and Dad can't stand the noise—TV blaring, toy trucks whistling. Kids are kids."

"What if you have other plans on a weekend?" I ask. I'm trying to discover whether Amanda sees that this arrangement might not be in the best interest of someone looking for a mate, but I won't say it directly.

"He would say I should tell him if I had something else to do and he'd stay home, but that has never happened."

Amanda notices something in my expression and adds defensively, "He tells me all the time that I shouldn't worry about him, that he won't come if I have other plans. I want my own life and I'd like to be in a relationship. I know he wants that for me, too. But as long as I can, why shouldn't I take care of him? I can always worry about my own plans later."

I see that Amanda is putting her life on hold, and she's been doing it for a long time—even before her mother died. I ask her what she wants to work on in the group, and she replies that she's not really sure—some feelings to resolve about her mother, that kind of thing. It's very vague. We'll wait to see what emerges, but I am pleased that she is eager to begin and is open to sharing. It will make a good start.

Irene starts sobbing almost the moment she sits down across from me. "I'm sorry," she says, embarrassed. "I promised myself I wouldn't do that." I assure her it's quite all right, and offer her a tissue.

I'm curious about Irene. At sixty-eight, she's a good deal older than most of the people who come to me— closer to the age of some of the parents for whom they are grieving. She's small and fit with thick gray hair cut

very short, and a warm, generous face. Her makeup is
carefully applied. Irene says right away she is very lonely.
She's a widow; her husband died of heart disease ten years
ago. Her only daughter, Roberta, who is forty-two, lives
in California, and she says she and her sixty-two-year-old
brother, Tom, don't communicate much, even though
they live near each other.

My impression of Irene is that she is lost and bewildered.
She tries bravely to control her crying and speak calmly.
"When I think of my father, I miss him so much. He was
ninety-two when he died—it's been almost a year now—
and he was at home with me, not in a hospital. He had
pancreatic cancer, but he fought against being in a hospital.
The doctor asked me if I could handle it and I said yes, I
could. I was very happy to do it."

"Was he sick for a long time?" I ask.

"Not really. He came to live with me after he broke his
hip four years ago, and I quit my job as a legal secretary
to take care of him. At the time, he was pretty healthy. It
was before the cancer was diagnosed. Everyone said he
lived like a king at my house, and it's true. A friend told
me, 'So, where's Robin Leach?'—you know, from *Life-
styles of the Rich and Famous*. I really pampered him."

"I assume your mother is not alive."

"No, she died twenty years ago, when she was about
the age I am now." Irene's face turns grim. "I wouldn't
allow myself to grieve for her when she died, but I col-
lapsed five years later and went into a terrible depression.
I don't want that to happen again."

"How did she die?"

"Oh, she had so many problems. She was diabetic and
grossly overweight. She died of a sudden heart attack—
can I ask you something?"

"Of course."

"I feel a little bit funny doing this. A lot of people have said to me I should be glad my father lived such a long life. I'm sure most of the people in your group are younger—am I right?"

I nod. "So . . . "

"So, maybe I won't fit in. Maybe I'm crazy to be making such a big thing of this. Ninety-two is a good age to die, isn't it?"

"You know, Irene," I say firmly, "when people make comments like that, they're usually trying to help. But whenever a parent dies, it's hard. I'll bet when people say ninety-two is a good age to die, you're thinking, 'Ninety-two? It's not long enough.' "

She nods vigorously. "Exactly. People don't understand that he was there for sixty-eight years of my life, and now he's not there anymore. My brother is annoyed with me. He keeps telling me I should accept it because Dad lived a long, full life." In the next breath, she cuts to the heart of things. "He doesn't understand that I've lost more than a parent. Dad was my companion for the last few years. His death has left a huge hole in my life. I liked being needed. I hardly know what to do with myself anymore."

Jane is a forty-two-year-old single woman who lost both her parents during the past year. She is the head nurse at a large metropolitan hospital. Her appearance and manner exude a wiry kind of energy. She is healthy-looking and slender, with short, severely cut black hair. My impression of her is that Jane is the kind of woman who seems to know exactly who she is and what she is doing. She has a guarded manner that comes across as confidence but also says, "Don't touch." However, in my office, she lets down her guard a little and admits that the death of both of her parents in the past year has shaken her to the core. Since she is an only child, she says she feels completely lost and without family. I ask her to tell me about how her parents died.

"Mom was sixty-five. She died almost exactly a year ago. She had asthma most of her adult life, and unfortunately, she didn't take very good care of herself, something that drove me crazy. I was always trying to talk to her about it, but she didn't want to hear my 'nurse crap,' as she put it. We were very close, but she wouldn't listen to me. About a month before she died, she had an attack that was so bad her usual self-medicating didn't work. My father took her to the hospital and when she got out, she came to stay with me so I could keep an eye on her and take care of her. It was very stressful for all of us, as you can imagine. She was a terrible patient. She just wanted to get up and leave. And she had a very difficult time administering the medication. I did everything I could, but I still had to work every day, so she was alone much of the time."

She pauses and wipes her eyes with a tissue. "This is very hard to talk about."

"I know." We sit quietly, and after a while she goes on. "One night, I returned from work to find her lying back across the bed. I could see immediately that she wasn't breathing. The oxygen tank was turned on and the tubing was around her neck. On the bedside table was a syringe with three or four vials of Adrenalin. It turns out that she overdosed. To this day, I don't know if she did it by accident or on purpose. It haunts me. I should have been there to take care of her. I play those last days over and over in my mind, wondering if I could have done anything differently."

She starts to cry again, and I give her a few minutes to compose herself. She seems very embarrassed, I imagine by both the tears and the revelation. "What you're feeling is perfectly understandable," I say. "It must have been a terrible shock for you." She nods and blows her nose.

"Tell me about your father. How did he die?" I ask.

She sighs. "He was diagnosed with prostate cancer only two months after Mom died. It had spread, and he went downhill very fast. My parents were very dependent on each other, even though they fought a lot. I'm sure his rapid decline happened because she wasn't there to nag him into living." She smiles a little through her tears. "He was only sixty-seven, but he seemed much older after she died. He died in the hospital, quietly in the middle of the night, and I wasn't there. I'd visited him when I went off duty earlier that evening, and I had no idea that he was so close to death. I was stunned when the hospital called me. I really started hurting when it sunk in that within a few months I had lost both my parents. I wasn't prepared for it. It felt like a horrible nightmare."

"Tell me what it's been like for you since," I encourage her.

"At first, I thought I'd be all right. I'm always all right. I'm used to comforting other people who lose family members. I've seen a lot of death. It's part of my job. But I can't seem to get myself out of this, no matter what I try. I keep going over it. Did my mom commit suicide? Did I do everything I could? Were my parents scared about being alone when they died? Am I going to be alone forever? These are the kind of questions that don't have conclusive answers." She wrinkles her nose distastefully. "I'm not sure I even want to know the answers. I try to keep it together at work, but at home I cry. No one wants to hear this. I'm tired of crying. I'm afraid if this keeps up, I'm going to lose my mind."

"You've got some big issues here," I tell her seriously. "Especially if you decide to explore your mother's potential suicide. The group will be a good place to start, but it might not be enough."

She nods in understanding. "Right now, I just want to break out of this misery. I'm used to thinking about other people, and I think the group will be good for me. Then, we'll see. . . ."

My first impression of Matt is that he oozes depression. He is a tall, heavy man who walks with his shoulders slumped in defeat. His face is pasty white and his eyes are bloodshot as though he hasn't slept for a while. A thirty-six-year-old computer programmer, Matt tells me his mother died four months ago. The last two years of her life she was very ill and he moved in with her to care for her. Now, he says, he usually keeps to himself. He is visibly reluctant about being in a group, because he says he isn't used to talking about his feelings. In my office, he shifts around in his chair as though he can't get comfortable, and tells me shyly, "My mother always called me her Rock of Gibraltar. She'd be surprised to see me now."

"Tell me about her," I say.

His face brightens. "She was a very intelligent woman— very unusual. Bright, witty, charming. Being around her was a delight and a challenge. My father died twenty-six years ago, and she has lived on her own and been very happy and competent. Some of my best times have been spent with my mother—and I'm not ashamed to say it. Even when I went away on business trips for my company, I called her every night from the hotel."

"So, she was sick for two years?"

"Actually, four years. She began to have heart problems when she turned seventy-five. My older brother, Joe, and his family have a big house, and she moved in with them— although I knew she would have been happier with me. It turned out to be true." His voice becomes bitter. "After she had been living with Joe for two years, she started to complain to me that he was abusing her. Not physically, but verbally. Being very critical. Making her feel unwelcome. That kind of thing."

"She told you?"

"Not at first. But when I found out, I couldn't stand it. So I convinced her to move to the country place our family has in upstate New York. I left the city to be with her, and basically dedicated myself to taking care of her until she died."

"It sounds like it took a lot out of you," I say sympathetically. "You gave up your life for her."

"No, she was sick and she needed me. I didn't mind." He pauses to wipe his eyes.

"How did your father die?" I ask.

"He died in an industrial accident when I was ten. My mother raised us alone, and she did the best she could. Joe always seemed to resent the fact that things were so hard. We never had very much money and we had to pitch in a lot as kids. When we got older, Joe couldn't wait to get out of the house. I never felt the same way. When she got sick, I was at her bedside every minute. The last weeks in the hospital were very hard. I watched her going downhill and there was nothing I could do to stop it. The day she died, I knew it would happen. It was like a sixth sense because we were so close. I spoke to her, held her, kissed her. She was in and out of consciousness, and when she opened her eyes, they looked vacant. I never knew if she heard me."

He stares at his hands. I ask, "And since she died?"

"Oh, I rose to the occasion when she was sick. I endured the most horrendous emotional upheaval without losing my sanity. But after she died, I fell apart. I never cease to be amazed that I function at all. Every weekend, I drive up to the summer house we shared and spend my time there alone, walking in the woods and reading. I know it's not healthy, but when I think about getting on with my life, as the saying goes, I can't imagine how."

I can see that his mother's death highlighted the dysfunction in his family. I wonder how his life came to be designed this way, how he and his mother became so interdependent. Was it his plan that she would never die and leave him? I tell him that further exploration will allow him to better judge how "healthy" his response is. "The issue is, what do you want to do from now on? If you want, you can learn some things about your family to help you better understand the way you feel. Then you can decide what to do next."

He nods, but doesn't seem to be very interested in what I'm saying. I can see it won't be easy getting Matt to open up.

Arlene is a beautiful, delicate woman, quite girlish. Although she is thirty-seven, she wears long billowing dresses and little flat shoes. Her thick blond hair hangs to the waist. Arlene's father died eight months ago, but he remains a potent presence for her. It has reached the point of crisis, especially since she is engaged to be married in the spring and can't shake her grief. "This should be the happiest time of my life," she tells me in a whispery voice. "But all I feel is sadness that Daddy isn't here to share it with me. He won't be walking me down the aisle." Her eyes start to tear at the thought. "He loved Greg—he's my fiancé. They had so much in common. My mother has tried to be somewhat involved in the wedding, but she's not the one I want." Her voice is petulant, and I wonder if she always sounds like a little girl when she speaks of her parents.

She goes on to describe a relationship of intense closeness, almost to the point of symbiosis. "Daddy was my only real friend most of my life. He was my companion and advisor. I followed in his footsteps professionally—he was an accomplished musician and when I was a child, I learned to play five different instruments."

"You saw each other often, I take it."

"Oh, yes, at least twice a week. We talked on the phone every day. He knew everything about me. Sometimes he could be critical, but I always thought it was for my own good. He was almost eighty, but he was as sharp as a young man."

"Tell me about his death."

"It was a complete shock. He had a heart attack; it was his second in the last five years. He was taken to the hospital and died after just two weeks. There were nurses around the clock, but until the day he died, I had no idea he was so sick. In fact, all along, I just assumed he would get better."

"And your mother?"

She frowns slightly. "My parents had been divorced for several years. She lives alone in Brooklyn, but she's been seeing a man there for a couple of years. Maybe they'll get married. I don't really know. My mother and I have never been close. I have a younger brother, Edward, who lives in Boston. He's always been my mother's child and I was Daddy's. After the divorce, Edward was so bitter that he stopped speaking to Daddy. He took my mother's side; he couldn't ever see her for what she was."

"Which was?"

"A selfish, materialistic woman. She never let up on Daddy about his music. She went on and on about how she could have married someone with a more stable profession. Money was an obsession with her. I think Daddy was relieved when she finally left him. She didn't even come to the funeral. Edward flew in from Boston, but he was very cool and he left as soon as he could."

"How old is Edward?"

"He's thirty-two. My mother is seventy-five. My parents married late in life. Edward is a professional man—exactly the kind of man my mother wished she'd married. Isn't that ironic?"

"Is it?" She just waves a hand as if to say, if I can't figure it out, she isn't going to bother explaining it.

"And now?" I ask her, changing the subject.

"I have no one to talk to about my grief, because no one loved him the way I did." She shakes her long hair dramatically. "Oh, what I would give for another year, another month, another day! We never even talked about the possibility of his dying. It never came up. He always liked to talk about solvable problems, and even though he must have realized he was in deep trouble, he never said a word to me about it. The thought of him leaving me, well, I was too scared to bring it up. So we never even got to say good-bye."

Arlene's feelings of abandonment are very real. Even her use of the term *Daddy* suggests that perhaps she never achieved the normal adult separation from her father. It makes me wonder about the circumstances of her engagement, so soon after her father's death. I'm curious to learn more.

"My mother loved me to death," Mary Ann tells me. She is a forty-five-year-old commercial artist, simply dressed in pants and a sweater. She wears no makeup, but her eyes are naturally dark and with her hair pulled back away from her face, she looks younger than her age. Mary Ann is married and has two children—a daughter, nineteen, in college; and a son, twenty-two, in medical school. She has a younger sister and two older brothers, and describes her relationship with them as distant. She also admits there has been a strain in her relationship with her husband and children.

"Even after I married and had children of my own, I was closer to my mother than to my own children or my husband, Steve. This is confidential. . . . "

"Of course."

"It would hurt them to hear that."

"They must have known how close you were."

She shakes her head. "No, no one could possibly understand it. Our relationship only grew stronger as the years passed. We always spent a lot of time together, but once the children left home, we became even closer. My father died of cancer ten years ago, so it's been just the two of us—and, of course, my sister and brothers. But my sister doesn't live in the area, and she and my mother never saw eye to eye. My brothers have their own lives and families."

"As you do," I point out.

"That's true, but it was different with me because of the special relationship my mother and I had. She once told me, 'I love all of my children, but you are my heart.' We talked six to twelve times a day on the phone, so you can imagine what a loss it is."

"I hope you had speed dialing!" I exclaim, and she laughs.

"I know it sounds like a lot. But it was natural. We enjoyed each other so much, and she needed me. She would have given her life for me. That's how much she loved me."

"What were your husband's feelings about your relationship with your mother?"

She shrugs. "Oh, you know, it's come up over the years. Sometimes when we were having a fight, I would call my mother or go to see her, and he didn't like that much. But otherwise, it wasn't really a problem. Until now. Now he thinks I'm off my rocker."

"He tells you that?"

"In so many words. His attitude is, it's been four months; get over it."

"And how do you respond?"

"What can I say? I think he's right. I just can't. I thought maybe your group would help."

"So, tell me how your mother died."

Her features sag and she looks momentarily lost. "My mother had been having health problems for several years—she was seventy-two. We took her to specialists, and she was treated to the best medical care for her angina. I thought she was doing better. Her death took place in June. Steve and I left the city to visit some good friends in the country for the weekend. I had promised to call her

Friday evening, but we were late getting back from dinner, so I never did. When I called her Saturday, she was furious about it. She'd been waiting for my call all evening. I was tired and I'm afraid I snapped at her. She hung up the phone. We spoke again Sunday, but she was very chilly. She died Monday. And that was that. Of course, I felt riddled with guilt."

I ask her why, although I can already guess what she will say.

Her eyes fill. "I didn't call her. Was it too much for her to expect that I could do such a simple thing? Then, instead of apologizing, I was irritated."

"I see." I want to say more, but it isn't the time. "So, in addition to feeling sad, you feel guilty."

She nods miserably. "People say, trying to be nice, 'Well, at least she didn't suffer.' But in my mind, she was suffering and I never got a chance to make it up to her."

Guilt can be a powerful force, and I know that when decisions are made from guilt, they will undoubtedly be misdirected and mistaken. I hope the group will help Mary Ann get more perspective and view the choice she made not to call her mother that night more kindly. I imagine there is much more to this story, and it will come out later in the group sessions.

"The experience of losing Papa is huge," Patricia tells me with deep emotion. "It never goes away. Nobody can feel your pain or know how much your parent is missed by you—nobody." She sits in my office, a thirty-four-year-old divorced woman, the mother of a five-year-old son. Patricia was born in Israel and her family moved to the United States when she was four. Her father, a survivor of the Holocaust, emigrated to Israel after the war and met her mother there. She has an older sister, also born in Israel, and a younger sister who was born in the United States.

Patricia is a darkly handsome woman with an exotic sweep to her hair, deep-set eyes, and a lithe, athletic body. She is employed as a fitness trainer at a city health club. She gazes at me with brooding eyes, filled with worry, and tells her story.

Her father—"Papa," as she calls him—was seventy-two when he died suddenly of a heart attack. His death occurred in February while her parents were spending the winter at their condominium in Florida. He died on a Sunday evening while he was watching television with her mother, and Patricia received the call in New York late that night.

"I always felt close to him," she says, "even though he wasn't a very open person. He had a quiet dignity and strength which I greatly admired. I leaned on him. And Papa was crazy about my son, Joel. In fact—" Her voice breaks, but she struggles on—"he wrote a letter to Joel on the day he died, which arrived two days later. Someone else read it to him . . . it wasn't me. I still haven't been able to look at it. Now, the hardest part is putting aside my own feelings so I can take care of my mother."

"She's still in Florida?"

"No, she came back to their house in Brooklyn, and she's selling the Florida condo. She doesn't want to go back there. Frankly, I don't know what she wants. She's only sixty-four and in good health, but she's lost. She was devoted to Papa and very dependent on him. In my heart, I know she will never get over this. She has almost stopped living and sometimes she consumes me with her sadness. I call her every day, but it's always with dread. She doesn't seem to understand that I'm hurting, too. She's incapable of comforting me. Every day I am reminded of what I've lost. Even if I could forget for a moment, my mother would bring me back to it. As long as she lives, we'll both be in mourning."

"And your sisters?" I ask.

"They help some, but it was always an unspoken agreement in our family that I was the one who took care of things. My older sister, Elena, has problems of her own. She functions all right, but she can't handle too much stress. My younger sister, Sarah, has always been the baby. That leaves me to be the strong, steady one. But this is too much for me. I worry that one of these days I'm going to crack—and then what will happen to my mother?"

She sighs in despair. "The worst thing is, I feel like I've lost both my parents, not just one. They were two halves of a whole, and my mother might as well have jumped into the grave after Papa."

Her face reflects the stress she feels. Listening to her talk is like hearing the sound of a dam breaking. Obviously, Patricia has kept most of her feelings pent up inside. At least with the group she'll have a chance to talk.

Eileen is thirty-five, plump and pretty, with curly blond hair. But her face is tense and unhappy. She is an elementary school teacher, married, with no children. She has an older brother and sister.

"I have to say right up front that I never felt my mother loved me," she says without preamble. Her tone is almost belligerent. "So why am I here? I want to figure things out about my screwed-up family."

"Screwed up—how?"

"My father was an alcoholic and that made our childhood very rough. My mother could never admit there was a big problem, although she suffered plenty at his hands.

My parents died three years apart—first my father from liver disease, not surprising. Then my mother six months ago from breast cancer. They were both seventy. Now it's just me, my brother, and my sister trying to pick up the pieces."

"So you're grieving for both parents."

"To be honest, I don't know how I feel about my father. I was ready for his death. He'd been sick for a long time and the doctors had told us there was no hope. The alcohol destroyed his liver. My mother's death came as a shock. There was so much between us that was unresolved, and now it never will be. I've been having a terrible time about this. After she died, I wore her rings for a while, but unfortunately, they gave me a rash, so I had to take them off. When my brother, sister, and I went to clean out her house, it made me very sick. I couldn't eat or sleep, and finally had to be hospitalized for several days."

"You had a very severe reaction to packing her things?"

"Yes, but my brother and sister thought I was being melodramatic. They were totally unsympathetic."

"What's your relationship like? Are you close?"

"You might say that. It's like we're bound together by an evil force." She laughs. "I know that sounds horrible. But when you grow up in a household like ours, things are confused. When we were kids, everything that happened depended on whether or not our dad was drinking. It was like a seesaw. We'd be OK if he was OK, and upset and afraid if he wasn't. I remember it like it was yesterday, but the strange thing is, my brother and sister seem to have different memories of the way things were. They've put it all away on a shelf, and neither of them seems too deeply affected by our parents' deaths. I'm the only one who is interested in working things out."

"Can you tell me what you think the issue is for you now?"

She surprises me with a very specific answer. "Oh, yes. My husband, Frederick, and I have wanted to have a child for some time, but I've kept putting it off. I always thought I could only do it after my parents were gone so I could start with a clean slate and not have my child subjected to all the rage in my family. But now they're dead, and I'm very scared because it seems like the rage hasn't gone away. My husband disagrees with me, but I really question whether or not it's possible to break the chain of pathological parenting. I don't want to be like my parents. I've been in therapy for several years. But after my mother died and I had such a severe reaction, my therapist recommended your group."

I'm glad to hear Eileen is in therapy. She's carrying a heavy burden. Meanwhile, I hope she finds the group a comfortable setting in which to explore further some of her family issues.

Richard is twenty-eight, a soft-spoken, handsome young man, newly out of law school, who admits he never imagined he'd have to face the death of his father so young. His father, also a lawyer, was only sixty-three when he died eight months earlier. "I have a six-month-old daughter and she'll never know her grandfather," he says sadly.

"Was your father's death sudden?" I ask.

"Yes. He had a stroke out of the blue, was rushed to the hospital, and died three weeks later. It took everyone completely by surprise. I'm having a hard time with it. I keep thinking that he never really had a chance to get to know me as an adult."

Richard admits that he is filled with conflicts about his

father's final days. He expresses what is called the "more-better-different" syndrome. "I wish I had done more for him while he was in the hospital. I went to see him every day, but I always felt guilty when I left—like I should stay longer. Even though he wasn't really conscious, especially in the last week, it might have comforted him to know I was there by his side. But it was too hard for me. When I went to the hospital, I'd want to leave almost as soon as I got there."

"What has happened since your father died?" I ask.

"Well, my older brother, Jim, lives in London, so the responsibility has pretty much fallen on my shoulders. Jim didn't even come and visit my father while he was in the hospital. He came for the funeral, then went right back. My mother, who is not in good health—she has severe arthritis—came to live with us. She's only sixty, and this living arrangement is supposed to be temporary, but who knows?" He raises his eyes to the ceiling in silent pleading. "I'm ashamed to say this, but it's been a pretty miserable experience. We never got along in the first place, and now she's there every day, criticizing and carrying on. So much has changed so quickly. I just became a parent myself, my wife, Sue, doesn't need this extra pressure—although she's been very supportive. I just don't know. Instead of being able to give of myself freely, I feel like I'm in prison—oh, this is really sick. . . . "

"We all have feelings we don't like. Tell me more about it."

He blushes a deep red. "I have crazy thoughts sometimes, like I wish she had died instead of him. He'd have been able to handle it much better."

"You're trying to deal with difficult problems," I say,

"and you sound like you're under a lot of pressure. It's the thoughts that you deny or don't allow yourself that are most destructive. You are attempting to figure out how to handle what's going on in your life."

"Really. . . . " He looks genuinely interested in this concept. "I never realized that. It's just that I'm only twenty-eight years old, and I already feel like I'm stuck. I don't want to spend the rest of my life tied down to a sick mother. So, I guess I'm here to deal with that, too. I know one thing: I can't go on like this."

"The death of a parent isn't a simple event," I tell him. "It always involves other relationships. You expect your reactions to be one way and when they're not, you become upset because you have unexpected and uncomfortable feelings. That's normal. Acknowledging those feelings is one of the main purposes of the workshop."

Helen admits that she's something of a control freak, and it torments her that her father died when she wasn't around to do anything about it. She is forty years old, a tall, thin, ascetic-looking woman who is married and has a two-year-old daughter. Her father died two years ago while she was pregnant. "Two years is a long time to be hurting so much," she admits. "I know I need help."

As she describes her family, Helen reveals that her grief for her father is complicated by a number of factors. Most important, she wasn't with him when he died. "He lived alone; my mother died when I was sixteen, and I was their only child." She corrects herself. "I should say, I was their only living child. I had a brother who died of leukemia when he was six. My mother was never the same after that. Anyway, I'm rambling. . . . "

"Not at all." To the contrary, this seems to me like pretty crucial material. But Helen wants to talk about her father.

"Usually, I tried to call or visit regularly, every day or so," Helen says. "But I was busy at work, my daughter had the flu, and it had been three days since I'd spoken to him. On the evening of the third day, after I'd put Caroline to bed, I tried to call him. There was no answer, which was strange, but I kept trying repeatedly. When there was still no answer by ten-thirty that night, I called a neighbor of his who had the key to his apartment. She asked me to hold the line while she checked. When she returned, she told me as calmly as she could that she was calling the police. I was frantic." Helen starts to cry. "I should have called him earlier . . . been there. I'm sorry."

"My guess is that you focus on 'not being there' a lot," I say. So much guilt in this new group of mine, I think.

"I can't get over it," she sniffs. "For two years I've carried it with me every day. I've withdrawn from everyone, even my husband and daughter. I can't tell anyone how I feel."

"Do you think it's gotten worse over time?" I ask her.

"No, not worse. There's just a dullness to everything. I'm usually a very happy person. I've lost my knack."

"Can you remember how it was when your mother died?"

Helen winces. "That's a whole other story! I could fill a book. Her sister came to live with us and she tried to be a mother to me. It was very confusing for a while, but then, life just went on. I do have one memory, of going to a school dance about a month after my mother died and feeling guilty because I was having so much fun." She turns thoughtful. "You know, I never really realized it before, but I never grieved for my mother. Life just returned to normal and we didn't talk about her much; my father was devastated and maybe I wanted to protect him. Who knows. It seems like a long time ago." She sighs. "Do you think the group can help me?"

I tell her, "If you let it."

Barry is a thirty-four-year-old government worker, stocky and boyish, with thick brown hair and very large blue eyes. His father died five months ago. His mother is still alive and healthy; she works for a travel agency. Barry has two older sisters.

"I guess I should have been prepared for Dad's death," Barry acknowledges. "He was a five-time melanoma survivor who was told off and on for twenty years that he only had a few months to live. But he defied the odds every time, so I came to think of him as somewhat invincible."

"How old was he?"

"Only sixty-four—he was so young! My mother is sixty-one. She's handling it better than I am, and so are my sisters, who are both great, strong ladies. It was actually my mom's idea that I come to this group."

"That's interesting. Why do you think she suggested it?"

"Of all my family, I seem to be having the hardest time with this," he says. "I'm the youngest of the three kids. My sisters are both in their late forties, so I was the baby. My dad was so thrilled to have a boy, and he and I were buddies. He was sick a lot when I was little, and we'd spend time together reading and watching TV and talking.

Anyway, part of the reason I'm feeling so bad is that I didn't stick around the hospital while he was dying." His smile fades and his eyes grow bright with tears.

"What happened?"

Barry takes a deep breath. "He'd been very sick in the hospital for about two weeks. Deep down, I thought this might be it, but I was hoping like crazy that he'd get over it, just like he did all the other times. Our family was big on hope. I went to see him the day he died, and he was so weak. I was alone in the room with him. My mother had gone out to get coffee. And he grabbed my hand and looked at me straight in the face, and his eyes were different. He said, 'I have to tell you, son, I'm scared.' Then I knew he thought he was dying. I'll never forget the way his eyes looked—watery and filled with panic. I was freaked. When my mother came back to the room, I made an excuse and left the hospital. I called my office and told them I wouldn't be coming in, then I literally fled to my apartment in Brooklyn and hid. What a coward, huh? He died later that day, and instead of being with him, I was curled up on my couch watching talk shows on TV."

Barry starts to tremble. "He was my best friend, and I ran away instead of staying to hold his hand and say good-bye."

"And you feel—"

"I don't know how else to describe it but heartbroken, and guilty that I wasn't there. My mother and sisters have all tried to talk to me about it. They tell me I'm being too hard on myself. But I can't find any comfort in their words." He pauses uncertainly. "You see, there's a complication."

I motion for him to go on, and finally he does, looking past me out the window as he speaks. "I'm gay—and I never told my father or anyone else in my family. I can't comprehend it myself—such a big deception when we were so close. I was afraid. But also, I always assumed the right chance would come along. I never imagined Dad would die before I told him. I imagined the scene so many times, from just about every angle possible. And now my chance is gone."

"And you believed there would always be time."

He finally looks at me. "I feel stunned. I want to chase after him and yell, 'Wait, I have something to tell you!' I hope this group can help me, because it's giving me a lot of problems and I don't have a clue how to deal with it on my own."

Marian's is the kind of story that makes you immediately want to reach out and give her a hug. She sits in my office, a twenty-three-year-old student, dressed in leggings and a long shirt with a pro-choice slogan emblazoned on it. Her face is round and pretty; her closely cropped hair makes her gray eyes seem large and striking. She clutches the edge of her chair and swings her leg in an agitated way as she describes the tragic circumstances of her mother's death, three months earlier.

"Mom was walking down the block outside our house— I live . . . lived with her while I'm going to college—and our neighbor Marge Gibson, who was a really good friend to my mom and me, backed her car out of the driveway without looking and hit Mom. She died on the way to the hospital. She was only fifty-seven. . . ."

Her voice trails off in shock, and I gently urge her to go on. "Where were you when this happened?"

"I was at school. My brother Jack—he's twelve years older than me—called the school and they came and got me in my history class and brought me to the office. All they told me was that Mom was in an accident. But then Dad showed up, and I really knew it was serious. They had been divorced for a long time and Dad was remarried. I knew he wouldn't leave his office and come to my school in the middle of the day like that if it wasn't serious. I started crying really hard as soon as I saw him.

"We took a cab to the hospital, and I still didn't know for sure she was dead, but I was crying the whole way. My brother met us at the emergency room and said she died in an ambulance on the way to the hospital. I thought I was going to pass out. Dad made me sit down and a nurse gave me some water. But it was all unreal."

I am deeply sympathetic. It is hardest of all to comprehend and accept death when it is so random and preventable. I can't help feeling a moment of regret that this young girl isn't somewhere laughing with her friends instead of dealing with this tragedy.

I smile at her and ask gently, "Are you still living in the house?"

She nods. "Yes . . . and trying to go to school, which is hard these days. Marge Gibson has been by a few times, but I have a hard time even talking to her. I know it was an accident, and I can't even begin to imagine what she must be feeling. But it doesn't matter. I can't be nice to her. Is that so bad?" Her big eyes are anxious.

"No, it's not so bad. This is a great shock, Marian, and you have to take care of yourself. I'm sure your neighbor is feeling a lot of pain, but right now, you can only do what you can do."

She looks relieved. "The thing is, I just can't accept that Mom's gone. Every day I read about people dying in accidents. I suppose thousands die this way. But my mom?

I want her to be back so much! I keep hoping maybe it didn't happen. Like the other day. I was lying on my bed, doing nothing, sort of daydreaming. It was the end of the day, the time Mom usually got home from work. I heard the door open and close, and the sound of her footsteps in the hallway downstairs. I heard her keys dropping on the table, then the rustle of her skirt as she went into the kitchen. They were the normal sounds I knew so well and they were as clear and real as ever. I jumped up from the bed and ran down the stairs thinking, 'She's home!' But of course, no one was there. The house was empty. It gave me the creeps. When I told my brother about it, he joked and said next time I see her, I should be sure to say hi for him." She makes a face. "I guess he was trying to be funny, but I felt stupid."

"Actually, it's not uncommon for people to have these kinds of sensory experiences when a loved one has died," I assure her. "Nothing to feel stupid about. Tell me, how's your brother doing?"

She shrugs. "OK, I guess. I never really know about Jack. He always keeps his feelings to himself. He's been taking care of all Mom's affairs since she died, and trying to decide what to do with the house. Dad's been OK, too. I know they're both worried about me, and I don't want them to be."

"Your loss is very recent," I tell her. "And the circumstances contribute to your feelings. Your mother died in a sudden, shocking way. I think being in this group will help you start to talk about it out loud. You sound like you haven't had the chance to talk about it very much."

"I don't want to upset my brother and dad. My friends are OK, but they all have their parents, so they don't really know what it's like."

"Each person in the group has a unique story to tell," I say. "But you all have something in common. That commonality can be comforting—you don't have to explain a lot. And I hope it can be healing, too."

These are the twelve people I am preparing to meet as a group for the first time. Although each person carries his or her special pain, they are not unlike others who have come through my group over the years. In the beginning, what they need most of all is to tell their stories. Almost always, the details—both large and small—of the loss of their parent are branded into their memories. Their stories pour out—the harsh descriptions of hospital rooms, an insensitive doctor or nurse, lingering illnesses, sudden crises, emergency calls in the middle of the night, unfeeling family and friends. Although death is the most predictable fact of human life, people are almost never prepared for it when it touches them so profoundly. While most adults expect their parents to precede them to the grave—it is the "natural order of things"—they feel stunned and abandoned when death occurs. The inevitable glimpse into the limits of mortality, the boundaries of natural law laid bare, terrifies some and discomfits all.

There seems to be no rational rhyme or reason to the emotional impact caused by a parent's death. The trauma is real whether the death follows a long illness or when a parent dies suddenly and without warning. It is traumatic when the parent is very old or when he or she is relatively young. Although most of the people in my groups believe their extreme grief is a sign of their greater devotion, this is not always the case. Grief can be equally intense—and even more so—when there has been alienation in a complex, lifelong relationship.

I think about all of these things as I prepare to join my group. In many respects, this work is like being a detective: collecting the information, figuring out how the pieces fit together, and understanding that every problem is really a solution to something else. I am always impressed with the willingness of people to let us look inside. After all, we only know what they choose to show us. But there is a lot of work to be done in the next six weeks.

CHAPTER TWO

THE EXCAVATION
OF A LOSS

He seems so near, and yet so far.
—Alfred, Lord Tennyson

Losing a parent has been referred to as the new mid-life crisis. Just as the "baby boomers" are beginning to hit their stride, attaining maturity, professional achievement, financial security, and personal peace—*WHAM;* the wind is knocked out of their sails.

It's not that we expect our parents to live forever. As we round the bend of forty, it's natural to start thinking about some of the challenges that lie ahead. Statistics show that by age fifty, more than 30 percent of Americans are full-time caretakers of their elderly parents. Every year, ten to fifteen million Americans experience the death of a parent. The signs are all around us; mortality is pressing in, but it's something no one wants to face. Even though the death of a parent can happen any time—indeed, several of my group members are young adults—it is in the middle years when the reality is most apparent.

As a society, we have trouble talking about death at all—

even when it's imminent. People have often told me about sitting in a hospital room over a period of days and weeks, watching a parent go into severe decline and then die, without ever mentioning the word *death*. Or of responding to a parent who says, "I'm dying" with denial—"Oh, no, don't say that. You're going to get better"—even when the evidence is clear. Then, after the parent dies, such people are heartbroken because, as they say, "I never had a chance to say good-bye." The missed chance was of their own making. It's as though by not uttering the words, they can prevent death from happening. But later, their sadness is heightened by the lack of closure.

Having said that, I also know that being prepared and talking about it doesn't necessarily ease the pain when death actually occurs. Losing a parent has a dramatic impact; it is different from any other loss for several reasons:

Your parents are irreplaceable. You've known them longer than anyone else in your life. They took care of you. You depended on them throughout your childhood, and that dependence may have continued into adulthood. You literally owe your life and your survival to them. Your relationship with them—whether you think it was good or bad—was totally unique. All other relationships can be replaced in some way. If you divorce, you can remarry. If you lose a friend, you can make another friend. But when your parents die, there is no replacement. You only have one mother and father. Even the word *mother* has a special meaning; to be mothered is to be comforted, cared for, embraced. When a parent dies, an emotional umbilical cord is cut.

Your relationship with your parents is the one upon which all others are based. Your family is where you learn about love, emotions, expressions, and expectations. It's where you are taught to be a social being. What you learn and practice with your family when you're growing up prepares you for a lifetime of relating. Every other relationship you develop is built in some way upon this foundation. You can learn a lot about yourself and your current interactions with others by examining the relationship you have had with your parents. There's always a connection, although it may not be obvious unless you examine your family's dynamics carefully. For example, a woman may describe her parents in glowing terms and say the relationship couldn't have been more perfect. Then she'll wonder why all her other relationships are so unsatisfactory. Chances are, if she explores the relationship she had with her parents more closely, she'll find important clues.

You believe in your parents' unconditional love. One of the most common themes that comes up in my workshops is the idea that a parent is the only person who really offers unconditional love—in other words, he or she would do anything, anywhere, any time for the child. To some extent, this is true, in the sense that most parents, even if they disapprove of a child, will always be there for the child. As the saying goes, "Home is the place that when you go there, they have to let you in." The expectation of unconditional love may be a comforting thought when your parents are still alive, but it leaves a huge hole when they die. It helps to view a parent's love in the proper context. Parents may love their children dearly but they are, after all, only human. Like other humans, they have their own needs that may have nothing to do with their children. Parents have private motivations, just like everyone else. And sometimes the affection given to children is not as unconditional as it seems. For example, we have to question the intentions of the "smothering" parent who encourages a child's dependency long into adulthood. Sometimes what looks like extreme love is really the way a parent meets his or her own needs.

People in my group invariably balk at this suggestion, as though there is something wrong about parents who consider their own needs. I know parents love their children. I also know that not everything they do is a result of that love. Sometimes their own needs take priority.

It is the myth of total, selfless parental love that often contributes to people's inability to comes to terms with a world that no longer includes their parents.

A parent's death is an encounter with mortality. Most of the people who come to my group are between the ages of thirty-five and fifty. This is a fragile time, because they are beginning to define themselves as middle-aged, and they experience some of the health problems and changes in appearance that come with age. They feel mortal, maybe for the first time. A parent's death only underscores what they're already feeling—that life comes to an end. The line moves up a generation, and they realize it is closer to their time to die. This increased feeling of mortality is seldom articulated or even realized on a conscious level. But it is there—a heavy weight on the subconscious mind. As long as your parents are alive, you can believe there is no end— like the woman who confided, "I never consciously knew my mother's age and I never asked her, because I wanted to believe she'd never die."

People say the death of a parent is the toughest thing they've ever faced. It causes emotional and physical collapse, dredges up guilt, and can spur dramatic change. Once a parent dies, you never have another chance to have the relationship you wanted. You feel regret for the missed opportunities, the absence of the parent in your life. People may try to comfort you, and even tell you it was for the best if your parent was very ill. But knowing something intellectually doesn't calm you. Logic doesn't reduce anxiety or any other strong emotion. The fallout cannot be avoided. There's no cure for death, and there's no cure for the pain of being a survivor—although that pain can ultimately lead you to make positive changes in your life.

The death of a parent leaves normally levelheaded people with their antennae raised for insult and injury. If you talk to people who have just buried a parent, chances are you'll find many tales about slights from family members and friends. They have exquisite memories for what others did or said. A woman in one of my groups simply could not get over her anger toward her mother-in-law. The woman came up to her at her mother's funeral, embraced her, and said, "Don't worry, honey, I'll be your mother now." Most likely the mother-in-law's intentions were loving, but that's not the way they seemed to this woman. "How dare she!" she exploded. "It was like a slap in the face. I just lost my mother. She can't be replaced." She has been unable to let it go.

Another woman told the story of how her father died at home when the two of them were alone together. He had a heart attack and stopped breathing. By the time the emergency medical team arrived, he was dead. At the funeral, one of her friends said casually, "I bet you wish you'd learned CPR." The comment sent the woman into fresh waves of grief and guilt, and she cut herself off from all contact with her friend.

A young man talked of having a close buddy ask him while he was sitting shivah (the Jewish rite of mourning) for his father, "So, what's your mother going to do with the house?" He told me, "That was it for us. I couldn't be friends with him anymore."

"My best friend from childhood couldn't make it to my mother's funeral," a woman told me bitterly. "My mother used to bake cookies for us when we were kids, and she was too busy to come!"

"I did everything for my friend Jeff," complained another woman. "Every time he needed support, I was there, just the way a good friend is supposed to be. But when my father died, he disappeared. He didn't even try to be there for me."

A man who sat by his mother's bedside every day for two months while she died slowly of cancer was told by a friend, "You're free now." He snapped back angrily, "Free to what?"

The acute sensitivity also extends to small gestures of kindness and acknowledgment. "I'll always remember the childhood friend who sent a letter when my mom died," a woman told me. "I don't even know how she knew about it, but she won a place in my heart forever."

These stories demonstrate the difficulty people have coping with the loss. Comments and behavior that they would normally shrug off are blown up to grand proportions. In calmer moments, they often worry about the extreme nature of their reactions, especially when they're negative. Do they have a right to be so mad at people who say the "wrong" thing? Should they forgive them? Is it worth carrying a grudge that could mean the end of the relationship? All of their reactions seem to be out of kilter, and they don't understand it themselves. But the impact isn't just emotional.

According to Debra Umberson, Ph.D., a University of

Texas sociologist who has been directing a long-term study of the responses adults (most of them in their forties and fifties) have to losing a parent, the impact of the event has a ricochet effect on all areas of life. Umberson reports that losing a parent places exceptional strain on marriages, relationships with friends, and work life. The death is an event that takes place in a moment of time, but it reflects the entire history of a relationship with that person and others around you. It's impossible to isolate it. For example, Dr. Umberson's research shows that in the months following the loss of a parent, there are greater incidences of spousal abuse, drunkenness, and extramarital affairs, as well as conflicts among siblings.

Sometimes the signs of grief are more subtle, especially with men. Men have greater trouble expressing grief than women. They have more invested in being stoic, in appearing not to be weak. Often their grief is expressed in more subtle ways. I think of the bright, athletic young man who let himself go after his father died. He dropped out of school, stopped working out, and gained fifty pounds. After we spent a few weeks investigating the changes in his behavior and appearance, he finally realized, "I had to let people know I was hurting, but I couldn't tell them. I felt like shit and I looked that way. I guess I was hoping they'd notice I was falling apart and help me without my having to ask."

Death doesn't impact everyone in the same way. Many people recover from the trauma in a short span of time. While the sadness may live in a corner of their hearts, they are able to move on. But if they don't process all of it, it will only look like they've resolved the loss. It may be years before it becomes obvious that it has been lurking inside, and even then, the connection between this death and a future event may not be apparent. The feelings associated with the loss may be deeply buried.

Others report an abrupt cessation of their essential happiness, as though a connection to the brain were permanently severed. This is most common shortly after the death. I recall once sitting in a group and listening to people talk about how they had forgotten what it felt like to be happy. The conversation started when one woman said, "My big question is, will I ever feel happy again?" This was a woman who had talked about being very much in love with her husband and having a delightful three-year-old daughter. In every visible sense, she should have been bursting with good feelings. But they were drained out of her. She feared the answer was: Maybe you'll never feel happy again. She had no sense that she could choose to respond differently by understanding why she needed to hold on to her feelings of sadness.

Predictably, everyone thinks death is easier for someone else. A bereaved daughter whose father had asked to be cremated and have his ashes scattered in the mountains, sobbed, "It would be easier if I had a grave to visit." Other comments I've heard include:

- "She has a husband and children to support her. I have nobody."
- "Her father was ninety. At least he lived a long life. My dad was only sixty."
- "It's harder for me because I'm an only child."
- "At least he had a chance to say good-bye. My mother died suddenly."
- "I know everyone thinks their parents were wonderful, but mine were exceptional."

And so on. Sometimes my groups can sound like the battle of the competing sorrows, a "Pain Olympics." People will say it's easier if you live nearby, or easier if you live far away. It's easier if one of your parents is surviving, or it's easier if you don't have responsibility for a surviving parent. It's easier if you have siblings, or it's easier if you don't have to deal with problems between brothers and sisters. It's easier if you don't have to go through your parent's things right away, or it's easier if you do. But the "Pain Olympics" only indicates that people don't think others really understand how hard it is for them. They don't feel heard, so they cry louder.

But pain cannot be judged by objective criteria. A parent's death is one of the most subjectively felt events of a person's life. There's no way to measure the trauma of the loss.

Just as there is no way to measure pain, neither is there a sure way to predict how an individual will handle a parent's death. However, experts who have studied the effects of death have isolated four major "risk factors" that might give clues. You can use these clues as a background to learning more about your own reaction to the death of your parents.

1. *Circumstances of the Loss* There is no hierarchy of shock when a parent dies, but your reaction might be different, depending on whether the death is sudden or happened after a long decline. Sometimes a long illness can prepare family members for the inevitability of death; they may be better ready to face it—indeed, even have reached a point of acceptance. On the other hand, a long illness creates tremendous stress in the family, and when death

comes, the members might be so exhausted from months or years of tension that they might be poorly equipped to deal with the event. And it can be complicated by other factors. A pregnant woman knew her mother was dying, but she was convinced she'd hold on until the baby was born. When her mother died a month before the birth, she couldn't believe it, so firm had been her hope. Another woman's mother died on the same day she gave birth. Even though the death was expected, the timing was heart-wrenching. "I didn't know whether to feel happy or sad," the young mother said, feeling torn in two by conflicting emotions. Forever, the two events would be linked with that day.

Sudden death, especially if it is violent, has been shown to have a larger impact on the survivors, simply because there has been no period of preparation. Random, meaningless, unexplainable deaths—such as being killed by a drunk driver, or being hit by a bullet intended for someone else—are the most difficult from which to recover.

2. *Amount of Social Support from Family and Friends* People who say they feel "orphaned" after the death of a parent tend to be more isolated than others. They are either only children, or are estranged from their siblings and other family members. They may have good friends, but for some reason, these friends are unable to provide support— or the mourners can't avail themselves of that support. One woman told me she thought she'd have an easier time because she had three close women friends. "I expected them to be more comforting. But I get the message when I'm talking to them on the phone that they don't want to hear about it. If they ask me how I am, they're hoping I'll say, 'Fine.' "

Similarly, spouses, who might be loving and supportive in the beginning, grow impatient if the mourner continues to be sad after the prescribed period. One woman reported that only two months after her mother died, her husband said, "I think it's time you snapped out of it." This isn't necessarily callous or hard-hearted behavior. It is difficult for people to watch someone else be sad and just let them be. It may be especially uncomfortable for a spouse who doesn't know what to do to help. Spouses also worry that the grief won't ever stop and they will have lost the "old you."

Death creates friction in a marriage because the person who loves you wants to help and protect you. He or she might feel that your inability to stop grieving is an issue of love: If you loved enough, you'd let your partner make it better for you. It's hard to convince a person who wants to "do something" that what can be done is let you express what you're feeling.

When your parents are divorced, it can also have an effect on mourning when one of them dies. There are complications in logistics regarding the funeral, and the event reinforces the fact that your family is "broken," only now more so. Also, the parent you might look to for help may have mixed feelings, especially if the divorce left many things unresolved. Their feelings may limit your ability to reach out to them and make you feel more alone.

Sometimes when the relationship with a parent is all-encompassing, the isolation is even greater. I began to see this with Matt when we talked before the group's first meeting. For two years, he closeted himself in a house with his mother and when she died, he had nowhere to turn for comfort. He couldn't get it from his brother, because he believed his brother was not as affected by his mother's death. He even admitted that he omitted his brother's name from his mother's obituary in the town newspaper to punish him for mistreating her, but also to highlight his own grief by declaring himself in print as an only child. That's a very defining act! (Of course, Matt never sent his brother a copy of the obituary, and since his brother lived in another part of the state, he probably never saw it.) Matt also isolated himself from friends and tried to deal with his grief by wallowing in it, making the house he had shared with his mother a shrine of mourning. In one sense, Matt did not want to be comforted or supported. He felt no relationship could ever be as meaningful as the one he had with his mother, and by keeping his grief alive, he could hold on to her. Deep down, and perhaps unconsciously, he believed that if he went on with his life, it would be a tremendous act of disloyalty to his mother. I knew after meeting with him that Matt would have a difficult time opening up to the group.

3. Mental and Physical Resources If the death of a parent occurs during a time when there are other major stresses, the impact is greater. A woman in one of my groups was upset because, in addition to losing her father, she also was responsible for paying the hospital bills, which were much higher than expected. This created a lot of financial stress. She said that every time a hospital bill arrived, it was like a stab to her heart.

One woman's divorce, the year before her father died, heightened her vulnerability to the loss. She told me, "I felt very sorry for myself after my husband left me. He stopped being involved in our daughter's care, so I had to carry the entire burden alone. I rarely went out for fun. Between work and child care, I dragged myself to bed exhausted every night. Then my father died. When that burden was placed on top of all the others, I felt suffocated by the stress. I literally had to force myself to slow down and breathe."

There is often residual anger if you were the primary caretaker of a parent during a long illness. Remember the way Irene, the older woman who was joining my group, described the way she cared for her ninety-two-year-old father? She said, "He lived like a king at my house." While on one hand it may give her comfort that she cared for her father so well, after he died, she seemed to feel some resentment that she gave up so much of her own life. Now she was very lonely. Who was there to give her credit for her sacrifice? Who would be there for her if *she* needed help? It will be hard for Irene to admit some of those questions and doubts.

Sometimes, even positive events can be stressful—like getting married, having a baby, or starting a new job. When a parent dies in the midst of a great change, it contributes to the feeling of uprootedness—like, "My God, is nothing stable?" Events that happen after death can also stir up sadness at the same time there is reason for joy. It's confusing, because people believe they're only allowed to feel one emotion at a time—either to be happy or sad. Most of the time, life is many feelings at once.

4. *The Nature of the Relationship* People in my groups almost always believe that the more a person loves a parent, the greater the trauma will be when the parent dies and the longer they will suffer. But relationships between parents and their children can be complicated. I saw this when I talked to the people in my new group. For example, Amanda admitted that her mother never approved of her;

part of her grief was the realization that she would never get a chance to win that approval. Likewise, Eileen, who grew up in a troubled family, believed that her mother's death unleashed a Pandora's Box of unresolved issues between her and her siblings. Another woman once said to me with absolute certainty, "I know if I had my mother for five more years, we would have worked things out."

Darlene's story is a good example of how much gets dredged up when a parent dies. Darlene was in my group two years earlier. Her case shows how the fallout from growing up in a family whose relationships are unhappy can reverberate long into adulthood. Darlene joined my group five months after losing her mother, to whom she was quite devoted. She was three months pregnant, and often spoke of how the birth of her child would give her greater peace about her mother's death. But when she called me two months after the group had ended, she sounded very upset. She asked if she could see me privately, and we set a date.

When she walked into my office I was startled to see how gaunt she looked. There was no sign of the blossoming beauty of pregnancy. Her face was pale and her eyes seemed huge and blank.

"Are you feeling all right?" I asked immediately. "Your pregnancy—"

She nodded sadly. "The baby is fine. It's me—I don't want him."

I sat back in my chair and observed her thoughtfully. Darlene's grief over her mother's death earlier that year had been somewhat tempered by the pending arrival of this child. But now I realized that she had always spoken of the child as though it were a girl. She had said, movingly, in the last session of our group, that she planned to name her after her mother as a way of continuing her mother's legacy in life. Now she was full of anxiety as she told me her fears.

"I was convinced I was carrying a girl. I knew it with every fiber of my being," she said. "But last month, I had an amniocentesis and they told me I was having a boy. I don't want this baby."

"Tell me why you feel so strongly about this," I urged her.

"I don't know." At first, she seemed confused. Slowly, we looked to her family tree for clues. What stood out was that all the men in her family were troubled, abusive, and out of control. Her framework for a mother-son relationship was based on this unpleasant picture. She thought it was safer to be a mother-daughter pair. Perhaps this had something to do with her strong response.

"All the men in my family are horrible," she said. "My father was an abusive man. My brother is abusive. It's like a genetic trait. I can't abide the thought of having a son who will carry that trait in him. I know I could love a daughter. I'm not sure I could love a son. Before I found out I was carrying a boy, I was so happy about the pregnancy. I don't feel happy about it anymore."

"Have you talked to your husband about this?" I asked.

"Oh, yes. He's furious with me. He thinks it's some kind of head trip, and I should just stop it. I know I'm ruining everything for him, but these dark feelings are not in my power to control." She went on to say that if her mother had been alive, it would have been easier to deal with. "My mother would have made it OK," she said longingly.

Darlene continued to see me during the following

weeks, and we investigated her emotional withdrawal from the child. She admitted that rationally she knew her reaction didn't make sense. But emotionally, she couldn't shake the dread. Many weeks of work with me gave her some relief.

Darlene's mental block was an extreme illustration of the way the parent-child relationship can have a profound impact on everything else. She possessed layers of feeling so complex that she couldn't reach the bottom without major excavation. Her unborn male child robbed her of a chance to replicate her mother-daughter bond, and forced her to reconsider her troubled feelings about her father. She thought they were safely buried and resented having to look at them again. It became her only real choice.

Even when a child is deeply devoted to the parent, the form that devotion takes makes a difference. The job of a parent is to help a child leave the nest and form meaningful relationships outside the family. So, although being helpful, always there, ready, willing, and able may look and feel like love, it isn't necessarily. It's as selfish to smother others as it is to ignore them.

Although it's easy to resent being ignored by a parent, it's often harder to see the problem with the parent who doesn't allow you to grow and achieve independence. People often speak fondly of parents who loved them "too much," who were overindulgent, who rushed in to ease the pain too quickly. This dependence is nurtured in the name of love, but that's not always what it is.

Thinking about my new group, I knew this issue would have to be addressed for several people: Mary Ann, who talked on the phone to her mother six to twelve times a day and said, "She loved me to death"; Matt, whose relationship with his mother was the only intimate one he'd ever had; and Arlene, who remained "Daddy's little girl" well into her thirties. I would gently push them to see the limits of such obsessive love, and help them find out if they felt they had permission to say no or to act otherwise if they chose to. They might say, "I never chose to act differently," or "Why would I?" But there's always more to the story. Mary Ann's guilt about not calling her mother the night shortly before her death would indicate that she never felt permission not to call.

I remember how a woman in one of my groups used to describe in glowing detail the close bond she shared with her mother. They did everything together. Her mother was her biggest fan. But I can still see her sitting in the group the day she was struck by a revelation, and wailing, "Why did my mother let me stay so dependent?"

I ask people who were extraordinarily attached to a parent who has died questions like, "Is this the legacy your father (or mother) would want—that you can never have a close relationship with another person? That you can't feel free to have a future that doesn't include your parent as your primary source of comfort?" This isn't restricted to people who don't marry or connect. Many married people describe their relationships in ways that indicate their parents still hold the primary place.

The attachment of a child to parents, especially to a mother, is essential to survival. The child is vulnerable; he can't function autonomously. It is believed this attachment is not just emotional, but biological and fundamental. With humans, the attachment is greater than with other species. Although most children become independent when they reach adulthood, the attachment remains on some level. Even for otherwise healthy adults, the death of a parent can stir up the primal fear of abandonment. But when you have a more integrated, balanced life, and have completed the normal transfer of emotional investment from your parents to others, it's easier to let go.

When I walk into a new group, I have several objectives. They are not always what people expect. Naturally, I want the people in my group to "feel better," to experience a healing of their sadness. But first I have to help them feel bad and learn to tolerate that feeling. Healing doesn't come without a process that is often painful. Our six weeks together is only the beginning of a long journey which they must continue after the workshop is completed. My goals for the six weeks are:

To give them permission to be sad. In the safety of that room, surrounded by people who understand what they've been through, they can relax and express their sadness without being judged. Out in the world, where the overwhelming pressure is to be normal, get over it, and be happy, they have perhaps sealed off their sad feelings. Expressing grief is an important first step to moving on. In my group, they can sit in a comforting circle, a full box of tissues at the ready, and express their thoughts and feelings without fearing censorship.

To help them view the relationships they had with their parents as they really were, not in an idealized way. Sometimes, when parents die, they become larger than life. But the highest tribute one can give the dead is to remember them as they were, not as one would like them to have been. I gently suggest that they look beyond the event of the parent's death, explore the entire relationship, and review the myths they carry with them. I help them see the consequences of long-term family dynamics and come to terms with the reality of their family and their own place in it.

To identify how their parents deaths have changed them. Only then can group members accept their changed selves, acknowledge the permanence of the loss, and begin to ask themselves the questions that will help them eventually restructure their lives. Often people refer to the death of a parent as splitting their lives in two: "There was BDD—Before Dad Died—and ADD—After Dad Died," was the way one man put it. "I saw everything through that prism."

To give them options. So often, people feel they have no choice about what they are doing. Maybe they want to do things differently, but they can't seem to find a way. I offer options that will help them become more empowered.

My workshop is about examining, scouting, finding new truths, and discovering possibilities. It is about challenging old scripts, tracking old feelings and ideas, reinventing directions, and replacing old thoughts and beliefs with new intentions. It's not about giving answers, but about asking questions. I invite people to embark on a grand excavation of their lives and relationships.

A wise man once said, "When something tragic happens, you can either shrink your heart and become bitter, or expand your horizons and use it to embrace life." This is the choice they have.

CHAPTER THREE

BEING SAD
TAKES ENERGY

While grief is fresh, every attempt to divert only irritates.
You must wait till it be digested. . . .
—Samuel Johnson

"People are always shocked by the powerful effect that sadness has on their lives," I tell the group in our first session together. "They think that they can overcome such a devastating loss and keep on going. They're surprised when they discover that their energies have been completely drained. What do you think? Does that sound familiar?"

The faces around me light up with recognition, and everyone nods. We are an hour into the first meeting of the group, seated in an intimate semicircle in the large, airy room the Y has provided. There's still a fair amount of shyness and hesitation, but I can see that most of the people here are beginning to loosen up and feel more relaxed.

It's one thing to talk privately with a therapist, and it's quite another to expose painful emotions in a roomful of strangers. But one positive thing has already occurred:

After an hour in which one after the other revealed the story of his or her parent's death, a part of the heavy burden that each of them carried into this room has been laid down. We have laughed, too—something most people don't expect to do, but somehow it seems OK in this room.

It's one of the best things about a group—the realization that you're not the only one on the planet dragging the weight of your grief around. Nothing makes people lonelier than to experience a crisis in their lives that no one else fully understands—especially when the pull from the outside world is so strong for them to be OK.

"But you can't go on as though nothing has happened," I continue. "It's impossible. The people around you might disagree, and you probably feel frustrated that you're not immediately capable of meeting their expectations, but you are in the grip of something very powerful. It helps if you compare the psychic pain you are feeling with what you might experience after you've had surgery. Surgery is an invasive procedure; your body is opened and then sewn back up. You're forever changed. Even after the scar fades, it's still there. It will always be there. And sometimes without warning it will begin to throb. After a parent dies, you are not the same, to varying degrees, and nobody should expect you to be. This is a life-altering event, and the lens through which you view the world has changed as a result. That's why some of you are finding it so hard to relate to people who are not in grief. It feels like they're on another planet." (Indeed the group members are most anxious to know if both my parents are living; they think it will give me far more credibility if I have shared their experience. I sidestep their questions for now, because this group isn't about me, it's about them.)

"It's normal to feel torn in two by your emotions and

to be uncertain about how to behave appropriately. After all, your responsibilities don't end when a parent dies. You still have to take care of your children, go to work, love your husband, relate to your friends. Life stops very briefly. And then, it's 'Put on your makeup and your tap shoes and go on stage.' Some people think it's preferable to get over a period of pain quickly and then try to go back to the way things were, as though there's a time limit to the grief you're allowed to feel. People have told me that if they go back to work and still seem upset more than a couple of weeks after the fact, their colleagues also become upset, but not in a supportive way. They'll even say, 'Well, if you have to cry, can't you just do it in the bathroom or something?' They either don't want to or don't know how to respond to such intense feelings. Even family members and friends get impatient and say, 'Are you still feeling bad?' It begins to feel like you're asking a big favor when you want to share something about your mom or dad. You start to think you're being a burden to others, so you keep quiet about your pain, but it doesn't change the way you feel. If anything, it just makes it worse."

I smile at the attentive faces around the circle. "People don't always know what to say. I recently met a woman who told me, 'I have a bad knee, and everyone has always had plenty of advice about my knee. But when my mother died, no one knew what to tell me.' That's why you're here. Everyone is going through a similar experience. You can talk about what you're feeling and express your sadness without being judged. And maybe being here will give you a fresh perspective; you'll feel less like you have to be what everyone expects you to be. You have a right to be sad, you have a right to seek help with what you're feeling. You have a right to take care of yourself in the most positive way that you can. So, we begin with where you are, not where anyone else thinks you should be."

"I know what you mean," Jane says. "My friends are always encouraging me to go out—they say it'll make me feel better. I don't think I'll feel better standing in the middle of a party somewhere, but I have a hard time telling them that. So I go along. But sometimes I feel there's a pressure for me to be OK for their sake—to make it more comfortable for them."

"How many others have trouble saying no when you want to?" I ask. "What Jane has described is a fairly common complaint."

"You feel like you're letting people down if you don't go." Jane adds. "I try to act normal with my friends so I won't be excluded, but these days, I don't feel too sociable. Sometimes I don't answer the phone so I won't have to say no. I feel more relaxed here with strangers than I do with my own friends."

"With me, it's a little different because I'm married," Helen says. "And I have a two-year-old. My husband is getting impatient with me. He says he's tried to be supportive, but enough is enough. Now I go into the bathroom when I want to cry, so he won't hear me. He does, though. He yells through the door, 'Are you crying in there?' Believe me, I understand. Who wants to be around me? But he doesn't have a clue what I'm feeling, because he has both of his parents. He even jokes. Tonight he said, 'Go to your death group!' "

"It's also the way people do things they think are helpful, but they're really not," Arlene interjects heatedly. "I have a close friend who is very attentive and wonderful. She's a good person, and I know she means well. She's always telling me if I need someone to talk to, she's right there for me. But it always ends up being her doing the talking. She's a terrible listener. I feel worse after I talk to her."

"Sometimes what you really need is someone who will listen," I suggest.

Arlene agrees. "I want to say to her, 'I don't need your advice about how to feel better. I just need you to let me feel bad.'"

"There's a reason people behave that way," I tell them. "It's quite stressful to let someone be sad. Even in this group, you will see people try to 'fix' each other. Most of us—and I think this may be especially true for women—are brought up to be pleasers and do-gooders. We learn to place a high value on making others feel good. Some people can't stand to see a friend in agony, and they'll jump through hoops to make the sadness go away. It's too scary, too out of control. We learn this very young. We fall down and say, 'It hurts,' and mother says, 'No, it doesn't.' Or 'It's not so bad. Don't cry.' You will see even here, where no one knew your parents, people will say, 'I know your dad didn't mean that.' It's just instinctive to want people to feel better."

"Then they blame you when their comforting doesn't help," Arlene adds.

"Exactly. So now you're the one on the spot, and because you were also conditioned to make people feel good, you want to comply by being—or at least pretending to be—less sad."

"I can relate to that," Amanda says. "I've always been the person in my circle of friends who people count on for support. Someone asks for help, and I automatically say yes without thinking twice. Just last week, a friend called and asked if I could stay with her two kids that evening while she went to a meeting. Her baby-sitter had canceled at the last minute. I couldn't . . . I just didn't feel up to it. It was one of the few times I've ever said no in a situation like that. Instead of understanding, she said, 'You're getting so self-involved.' I was outraged. I yelled at her, 'How can you say that? I just lost my mother!' But I can tell she didn't get it. She said, 'You didn't *just* lose your mother. It's been six months.' " She sighs and looks miserable. "I should have said yes. I didn't have anything else to do."

"Yes, you did." She looks at me in surprise. "Just because you didn't have formal plans doesn't mean you didn't have something to do. Your plan was to take care of yourself that night."

Patricia, seated beside Amanda, pats her on the arm. "I know how you feel. I handled all the details of my papa's funeral and took care of all his affairs, and everyone kept congratulating me for being so strong. It made me proud— I was such a little trouper. But then it started making me feel resentful; it was all just too much. Why did I always have to be the one to be strong and handle everything? Why couldn't anyone see that I wasn't so strong? I was hurting a lot, too, and feeling awfully vulnerable. But nobody was there for me, because they needed me to be there for them."

"Did you ask?" I wonder. "Sometimes people forget to ask."

"People who say they're your friends should know what you need," she responds defiantly.

"*Should* should be a four-letter word," I say.

Patricia laughs. "OK, you're right. But it's hard for me to ask. I'm afraid they'll be disappointed in me, because I usually do so well in a crisis."

"Some of us invest a lot in being strong and capable," I remind the group. "I suspect from what I've heard so far that there are a few people like that in this group. You may want desperately for someone to be there, sympathize, listen, or just give you a hug. But the signals you send out relay the message: 'Don't worry, I have everything under control.' You have to question what satisfaction you derive from being overly responsible and appearing to be so strong. The concept is called secondary gains. You perceive on some level that there is a benefit to your behavior."

"I suppose I'm guilty of that," Richard admits. "I have a wife, a baby, and now a sick mother living with me. If they think I'm cracking, they're going to be pretty upset. As it is, I spend half my time comforting my mother and the other half comforting my wife since her life has been so disrupted by my mother moving in."

"I'd like to remind you all of something you may know is true but have forgotten," I tell them. "That is, sometimes people who love you want more than anything to be able to help you; you think you're doing them a favor by sparing them your pain, when really the opposite is true. If you let them help you, they may feel closer to you. Patricia, I'd like you to think about that, and you, too, Richard. You may be missing an opportunity by trying to stay so strong."

Around the semicircle, faces are relaxing as these revelations are made. I have great empathy for these men and women who are fighting daily against a confusing jumble of internal and external needs. But I can see they are growing less visibly anxious as they listen to what others have to say.

"So," I ask them next, "with everyone around you trying to act like life is the way it used to be, what have you done that demonstrates to you that it's changed?"

A number of people in the group are quick to talk about the differences in their lives.

"I have never been a religious person," says Jane. "My parents took me to church when I was young, but I stopped going after I grew up. Then, when they died—I don't know, it seemed so inconceivable to me they could just disappear. I started thinking about the old days, the times we went to church together, the hymns we sang. It was a combination of nostalgia and soul-searching, I guess, but I've started going to church every Sunday. I like it. It's comforting."

"I'm doing something very specific," Arlene says, on a different note. "I've started a malpractice suit against Daddy's doctor. It's something I have to do—a way of seeing that justice is done."

I'm a bit surprised to hear this, since Arlene failed to mention it in our private meeting. "Why are you suing?"

"I honestly believe Daddy's care was mismanaged," she says angrily. "They didn't act quickly enough. To add insult to injury, the hospital staff showed a total lack of concern. I'm very angry about it. These were the last days of Daddy's life, and not one nurse or doctor stopped to comfort him. He was left alone almost constantly in that cold, sterile environment. The day he died, he was in great pain and having trouble breathing for hours. I couldn't get the doctor on the phone. When his heart stopped beating, they called a Code Blue, and doctors and nurses poured into the room. They pushed me out into the hall, and I stood there getting more and more hysterical as I listened to them whacking his chest and giving him jolts of electricity. After he died, they wouldn't even let me sit with him. It was unconscionable behavior, and I believe Daddy might be alive today if his medical care had been handled more responsibly."

Arlene's case may or may not be legally sound, but from an emotional standpoint, it's understandable. When people in my groups describe their parents' hospital experiences, they are often bitter. Even when they know rationally that the doctors and nurses were doing the best they could, the sight of their mother or father lying in a cold hospital room, surrounded by instruments and connected to tubes, cared for with the sometimes abrupt efficiency typical of hospital personnel, is very upsetting. Their anger is heightened by dashed hopes, and they want to blame someone. They tend to view doctors in a childlike way, trusting that, armed with sophisticated technology and secret medical knowledge, they can be omnipotent. When doctors fail to produce the miraculous recovery, it's easy to compress the grim events leading to death into a horror story of mismanagement and malpractice.

"Whether or not there is actually malpractice, most people respond to a parent's death with the sense that a terrible injustice has been done," I say. "That's normal. But whether or not there is injustice involved in your loss, it's the loss itself which is at the crux of your feelings. Some of you may feel tremendous anger now, and taking action—any action—makes you feel better. It's not an unusual way to channel some of the strong feelings. It gives you a purpose that relates to and memorializes your parent."

Arlene blinks at me uncertainly and twists a long strand of hair in her hand. "My fiancé, Greg, is a lawyer. He thinks I have a strong case."

I know she wants to hear my opinion of the merits of her suit. She's looking for legitimacy. I smile noncommittally and ask, "Anyone else?"

"I have a lot of stuff in my head about my parents," Eileen says. "I don't know whether to be more resentful of my father because he was drunk and abusive, or of my mother because she let him get away with it. I've really been working on my anger, but it's definitely my strongest feeling right now."

"If that's your feeling, listen to it," I say. "Examine it and see what's there. When you say you're working on your anger, it implies you're trying to get rid of it. Maybe what you need to do is bring it out so you can discover what it means. There is a difference between controlling or managing your anger, and understanding the impulse behind it."

"If I'm angry at anyone, it's at myself," Mary Ann says quietly. "Because of my selfishness, my mother died unhappily. Maybe I even hastened her death."

"You're talking about the night you didn't call her?" I ask. She has already repeated the story to the group.

"Yes." Her eyes fill with tears and she grabs for a tissue from the box in the middle of the circle. "Was it too much for her to ask that I spend fifteen minutes on the phone with her every day?"

"Maybe it was," I say mildly. She frowns at me as if she can't quite comprehend my point, but doesn't say anything else.

"You feel guilty," I add. "Guilt is a very common emotion for people who have lost a parent—even when they were dedicated sons and daughters. Your mind floods with thoughts of blame. You can't let go of that one night out of hundreds or even thousands of nights when you did call. And now you've convinced yourself it might have made a difference. It's a tape playing over and over in your head. Do you think your mother would still be alive if you had called?"

Mary Ann looks confused. "I . . . I don't know."

"That's my point. You can't know. It's your choice where you put that phone call in the scheme of things. You can use it as a reason for self-blame, or you can examine why that call is such an important event for you."

"I guess I've felt guilty about not spending more time with my dad when he was sick," Richard says. "He never liked being around sick people, and I think I inherited that attitude from him."

I notice Barry is wincing as Richard speaks. From what he has said, I'm pretty sure he's feeling the same way. He'd expressed so much guilt about leaving the hospital before his father died.

"Sometimes anger can actually make you feel better," I observe. "It's an easier feeling to grab on to than depression, because it's active. It keeps your adrenaline going, you can feed off of it. Depression is different. It's more passive and all-pervasive. It drains you of energy and robs you of the desire to perform the simplest tasks. It deprives you of pleasure, even for the activities you once enjoyed."

"That's where I am," says Matt sadly. "I go up to our cabin on the weekends and I feel a brief comfort from being there, but then what do I do? My whole reason for being there is gone. I feel lost."

Arlene shakes her head dramatically. "Oh, yes! Who can possibly understand what it's like to no longer have this person there who was your whole life?"

I let her description of her father as her "whole life" pass for now, although I'm tempted to ask if her fiancé knows this. We'll get to it later, I'm sure. I nod to Jane, who has raised her hand.

"I know I don't have the energy I used to," she says. "My life goes on day after day—I'm on automatic pilot. I put one foot in front of the other and go to work at the hospital, do my laundry, feed my cats. I probably look the same on the outside, but inside I feel dead. Nothing gives me pleasure anymore. People keep telling me this is temporary, but I'm not so sure."

"I'll tell you how I know I'm depressed," Irene adds. "My house is a mess. I've always kept it spotless, but not lately."

"You're making a good point," I say. "Sometimes these mundane, practical changes seem to be the most meaningful."

"I was always such a neatnik," Irene persists. "It was my claim to fame."

"It helps to observe your behavior over a typical week," I suggest. "See if there are things you do differently—like letting the house get messy. Then ask what can give you permission to let it be that way."

"I don't know what category you would put this in, but ever since my father died, I have found myself secretly reading the obituaries every day," Barry says. "I never paid any attention to them before, and I would feel embarrassed if anyone knew about it. It sounds so ghoulish. I spend a lot of time with them. I look for deaths of people who are older, and I wonder why those people lived so long when my father died so young. Then I notice if they are survived by children. If they are, I wonder if those children are as upset as I am. I feel bonded to them—like I could walk up to any one of them and we'd have something to talk about."

I laugh. "Which is really what you're doing here, isn't it? Until tonight, everyone in the room was a stranger to you."

He chuckles. "That's right. I never thought of that."

"I do the same thing," Amanda says. "Read the obituaries and make up things about the people." Others in the group are signaling their agreement.

"This is interesting. How many of you read the obituaries now?" I ask.

Several hands go up—nearly everyone.

"You say you feel bonded to these strangers. Let's talk about that."

"It's as though we belong to a club," says Helen. "The Dead Parents Society." This brings a laugh.

"And you think no one else can understand—"

"No one can," Jane says fervently. "Sometimes a friend will say something sympathetic and I just want to scream, 'Who are you to say anything? You have both your parents.' "

"I walked in here tonight," Matt says shyly, "and I was very nervous about coming. But I'm surprised by how comfortable I feel. I know these people. They've lost parents, too. They're not going to shut me out."

The group bursts into a spontaneous bevy of shared confidences. And with that, their true journey begins.

I once heard a seventy-year-old man at a conference describe his pain over his mother's death thirty years earlier in this way: "When my mother died, I felt awful—like I had this huge hole in my heart. Over the years, scar tissue built up over it, and in time, it stopped hurting every day. But certain people, like my wife, know where that tender spot is, and when they touch it, the pain floods over me like it was yesterday."

I tell this story to the group when we meet for the second time, as a way of illustrating the profound and lasting effect of loss. Also, to reassure them that when the pain stops, they won't lose the connection with the person who has died. This story reminds them that even at the point when their pain is no longer a constant presence, they'll still carry the person inside.

During the first session, we talked about how hard it is for those who are in mourning—how eager people are to diminish the change and make everything just the way it used to be. Now I ask them to touch those soft spots—to talk about what happens when they remember. "Time eases things, but time alone doesn't heal," I say. "There are still tender spots that can be activated unexpectedly with a word or an incident. Tonight I want to talk about where those tender places are for you."

"My son Joel will say something cute or do something wonderful, and I'll pick up the phone and call Papa without thinking," Patricia says. "Sometimes I dial the complete number and my mother answers the phone before I realize what I'm doing. Then I have to talk to her." Several people in the group snicker appreciatively. Patricia has told us how hard it is to talk with her mother these days. "It always makes me feel bad. Papa was the person I shared these things with. He got such a kick out of hearing about Joel's escapades. Sometimes I'll think of him and say with shock, 'Is he *still* dead?' "

"When my daddy was alive," says Arlene dreamily, "I used to be able to go home and be his little girl. I know that sounds silly. I'm a grown-up woman. But I felt safe when I was with him. Now I have nothing that gives me that feeling of safety. When Daddy died, all the links to my childhood were broken. It makes me feel so alone to be without him."

"Yes," I say. "It's especially difficult when you think you are feeling better, and then something happens and it feels like you're back to square one. The road is windy."

"All it takes for me to be jolted back is for someone to say, 'I'm going over to my parents' house,' or 'I have to call my mom tonight,'" says Matt morosely. "Oh, that hurts! It's like I've been stabbed. I almost had a breakdown recently listening to a guy at work talking to his mother. You know that patronizing tone some people take with their parents? It sounded like he was talking to a bad child. I couldn't stand it. It doesn't seem fair that someone who hates his mother still has her, and I loved my mother so much and she's gone."

"It's a roller coaster," Mary Ann says tiredly. "I'll get up some mornings and think I feel OK, that I'm getting better. I'll be having a good day, feeling strong. Then someone will make a comment or I'll see a TV show— and suddenly I'm thrown right back into feeling shaky."

"That scares you," I observe.

"Yes, it does. Last week you were talking about how it was like surgery, and I thought that was a helpful image, because it's exactly like that. I had a caesarean when my daughter was born, and I came through it pretty well, but every once in a while, I'd wake up, months or even years later, and barely be able to move. It was maddening. This feels like that."

"That's a good image," I tell her.

"Of course, once I get started thinking about my mother, I'm lost. I start feeling, 'If only—'"

"Ah, yes," I interrupt. "The 'if onlys.' Everyone has

them. 'If only my father had let me take him to the doctor.' 'If only my mother had listened to me.' Unfortunately, you can't change one event or behavior without making the entire relationship different. That's the way life is." I look around the room. "Someone else?"

Richard says, "What's different for me is that my father was the buffer between my mother and me. She and I have always argued a lot about everything, and he had such a way of soothing ruffled feathers. Dad could have been a Middle East negotiator—that's how good he was. Now, my mother and I circle around each other, afraid that an argument might break out. We can't seem to talk about anything. Every subject is off-limits—especially the subject of my father."

"Maybe not having your father as a buffer will change your relationship in ways that surprise you," I suggest to Richard.

"I doubt it," he replies gloomily. "You've never met my mother. She lives to argue."

I pick up on what Richard says to tell the group, "Everyone has their family systems—the predictable ways people behave. But one of the consequences of a parent dying is that the family system changes, and the roles other members play shift around. People take up the tasks and roles of the dead parent. Sometimes that's for the good; sometimes not. But don't be surprised, Richard, if you find your relationship with your mother evolving in unexpected ways. We'll be talking about that more later. Anyone else?"

"I had kind of a funny experience last week," Amanda says. "Before she died, my mother called me quite often, and I tended to see it as nosy. If I wasn't home when she called, she'd want to know where I was, who I was with—

hopefully a man—and what I was doing. I'd get offended and tell her, 'It's none of your business.' Sometimes I was pretty rude. So now, my father is doing the same thing, but instead of thinking, 'Why does he have to be so nosy?' I'm thinking, 'Isn't this touching. He cares about me.' "

I feel like congratulating Amanda. This is the kind of self-revelation that can be useful. "Why do you think there's such a difference?" I ask.

"It was part of the dynamic my mother and I had all my life. She would be pushy and I'd withdraw. It was like a reflex action. But I guess deep down, I counted on her to worry about me. Even when I got annoyed, I knew she'd keep doing it, so it was OK. Now she's not there to nag me and—" she stops to rub tears out of her eyes— "my dad is all I have. I appreciate him more. It's nice we worry about each other, but sometimes I feel like I've replaced my mother. He used to tell her all his activities. Now he tells me."

"As I mentioned, I've started getting more religious," Jane says. "For example, I always thought I'd be cremated, but now I want to be buried beside my parents; there's an extra plot. Then we'll all be together. It gives me comfort to think of lying there beside them, and I have growing faith that there is an afterlife we can share. Sometimes—I know this sounds gruesome—I think I'm just biding time on this earth until I can join my parents."

There is a rustle of discomfort in the group. It is a dramatic admission.

"Oh, you don't really mean that! You're young—" Irene starts to protest.

I hold up a hand to stop her. "It's hard sometimes to listen without trying to give advice, isn't it? But I'm going to ask you to try. You know," I tell them earnestly, "in this room, people are free to reveal their most private thoughts. Sometimes they say things they've never said to anyone else in the world—including family members. It's more helpful if you curb your desire to 'fix' things for each other. It's a common instinct to make nice, but it puts a period on a conversation. We want people to express more of what they feel, not less."

Jane smiles through her tears. "I'm sorry. I didn't mean to be so melodramatic. I don't really think there's nothing left for me in life; if I did, I wouldn't be here. It's just that—sometimes it doesn't seem very clear what will make me happy again."

I nod in understanding. "Uncomfortable feelings are OK."

"I . . . I welcome those sad moments when I most miss my mother," Matt says quietly.

"That's interesting," I encourage him. "Why so?"

"I'm not saying I think it's healthy. I realize I have to stop being so obsessed. But deep down, I'm afraid if I stop hurting, my mother will really be gone for good. Because I remember her and hurt, she sort of stays alive."

"You're not ready to feel better," I say gently. "Sometimes it's not so much the fear that you won't survive without your parent, but the knowledge that you will."

"I don't want to lose her completely," Matt admits. "Not hurting would mean that to me."

"There's nothing wrong with hurting," I say. "It's not good or bad, normal or abnormal. It just is. Some people hurt every day for a long time. Others don't feel the hurt in the same way. I notice, Matt, that you often refer to your reactions as 'healthy' or 'unhealthy.' Have you always put labels on your feelings? That's another way we have of stopping ourselves from learning more. If you say,

'That's good, bad, or stupid,' it doesn't help explain anything. You might use your observation about grief to push
yourself a little. Maybe try to imagine where you would
be if you didn't have the grief about your mother's death
to occupy your thoughts. Over time, this might help you
accept the permanence of your loss and make some different decisions. Such as, what would you have to do if
the grief didn't immobilize you?"

I address the group. "The most important work we have
to do together is to learn to ask questions as a way for you
to consider new possibilities and explanations. We'll examine whether or not your deep feelings of guilt or despair
are stopping you from doing the other things you want
to do in your life. Then, you have to decide whether or
not you want to make a change now. Our purpose here
is to open doors and help you begin to make that evalu-
ation. You may decide that what you're doing is all you
can do now—like you're stopped at a red light, but you
know it will turn green later and then you'll move. Or
you may discover that there's another way for you to deal
with what's happened. Which brings us to your assignment
for next week." They look surprised, and I tease them,
"Yes, we have homework here. Next week, we want to
move away from the event of your parent's death and talk
about your memories from the past. So, think about it
during the week and bring one memory of your parent or
parents to share."

"Good or bad?" asks Eileen immediately.

"It doesn't matter. We're just gathering information.
The memory you choose will tell you something."

"Should this be a memory that captures the total person?" Arlene wonders.

"Not necessarily. It might be anything. With one group

I had, every single person had a memory that took place around a meal. The point is that I want you to start considering the history of the relationship you had with your parent while he or she was alive. Sharing memories is a good way to begin. You might find the assignment hard. Just do your best. There are no grades here."

They leave the session chatting among themselves like old friends. As always, I am amazed how fast intimacy develops in groups. It is analagous to the tight bonds that get established among soldiers in war—as though their entire life stories have been condensed and assimilated in a couple of hours' time. They are still feeling too hurt to see it, but I consider this one of the miracles of human endurance. Life goes on.

After the group has met twice, I consider what has occurred so far. The first two sessions often sound like a testimonial dinner, a who-can-top-this-one of lavish praise for the deceased parents, combined with the "Pain Olympics" of their own grief. Those who are more openly ambivalent tend to say less during those conversations, not wanting to expose themselves as the only ones who didn't have perfect parents—or, worse still, as the only ones who weren't completely devoted. I've noticed that Eileen, whose father was an alcoholic and whose mother was an enabler, has said very little during the first two sessions. When she has spoken, her tone is so bitter that the others seem helpless to respond. When we begin to examine the past, I will encourage her to speak more. The truth is, there are more people with ambivalence in the group than is yet apparent. Ambivalence demands that each of them accept in one person the "good" parent and the "bad" parent—as one and the same person. This is very hard to do. But I've seen glimpses of the seeds of this struggle, even in Mary Ann, with her suggestion that her mother seemed to stand in the way of a healthy relationship with her husband and children. Jane is clearly troubled about the cause of her mother's death. I know she's struggling to come to terms with the possibility that her mother committed suicide. Amanda has suggested several times now that her relationship with her mother was volatile. So far, much has been said, but more has been left unsaid.

Then, of course, there are Matt and Arlene, who are determined to glorify their parents. I'm not in the business of knocking beloved parents off their pedestals for the fun of it. But I will try to help Arlene and Matt see that it's OK to acknowledge their parents as human.

Marian has said little, and seems very shy, often staring at her lap and swinging her leg in that nervous way she has. I've let her be silent, thinking perhaps what she has needed up until now is to listen, not speak. The circumstances of her mother's death were so shocking, she'll take extra time to reach a point of acceptance. Over time, her recovery will be helped the less she observes and the more she participates.

Next week, when we begin to explore memories, it will be a mixed bag. It's natural to cherish the good memories, since they can be so comforting. Besides, there is a cultural taboo against speaking ill of the dead. Many people feel disloyal about revealing oddities, eccentricities, or even cruelties. Others have the opposite struggle. They are determined to see only the negatives, as though if they admitted love, it would make them hurt more.

What I know is this: Every parent-child relationship contains a complex story of a life-long journey shared together. Sometimes they were in sync; sometimes their paths diverged. Often things appeared one way but were really another. Secrets were kept; hurts and resentments were never divulged. In most families, events from the past are stored in bank accounts where they've accrued interest for years or even decades.

The understanding of these complexities is every bit as crucial to the healing process as are the surface recollections. This is what I want the group to begin to consider when we meet again.

CHAPTER FOUR

THE MYSTERIES OF GRIEF

We live by losing and leaving and letting go.
And sooner or later, with more or less pain,
we must all come to know that loss is indeed
a lifelong human condition.
—Judith Viorst

A few years ago, I had a woman in my group who, although almost thirty-seven, had never experienced the death of someone close to her—until her father died. "I'd never even been to a funeral," she confessed, almost sounding embarrassed by her lack of experience. "My first reaction when my father died was, 'I don't know how to do this. Help!' "

She described feeling adrift on a tide whose course and destination were unknown. "During the days following his death, I watched the way everyone else was reacting. My sister was a puddle; she couldn't stop crying. My mother was in shock, dazed, on the point of collapse. I thought she'd crumble and disappear at any moment. So, this was what grief looked like, I thought. But when I looked in the mirror, my face was a mask. I saw nothing. I felt coldly detached from the entire event. I wondered— shouldn't I be crying like my sister? Shouldn't I look pale and fragile like my mother? Their grief seemed somehow larger and more important than mine. I felt guilty and confused."

Months later, just when things were settling down in the rest of her family, she fell apart. It was at that point when she came to me. She was terrified, because she didn't understand and couldn't seem to control what was happening to her.

"I don't know where these feelings of anger and depression are coming from," she said. "They've appeared out of the blue. Suddenly, I find myself thinking about my father all the time and crying every day. My reaction doesn't fit with what I'm seeing in others. My mother and sister, who were so devastated in the beginning, seem to be getting on with their lives. And look at me!"

She sighed unhappily. "Of course, everyone thinks I'm putting on a show. The 'authorities' in my family have announced that the grief period is over and they expect me to fall into line. Well, it's just starting for me, and I can't."

This woman was experiencing the unpredictability of the response to loss. She had a delayed reaction, but the reaction came, nonetheless. You can't be sure how you're going to react to a parent's death until it happens. Each loss and each person's reaction is different. You may have lots of symptoms—dizziness, sleeplessness, headaches, numbness, chest pains. Or you may not seem to be grieving at all.

When your parent dies, you enter into unfamiliar territory. It is not uncommon to feel lost, confused, and estranged from the rest of the world. Although there are some guidelines for recognizing and handling grief, you may have trouble understanding or describing what is happening to you, because it's all new. The most common question people ask is, "How long will I feel this way?"

The ultimate goal of the work I do is to guide people through the period of grief and to help them move past the emotional fever of mourning, come to some degree of acceptance about their loss, and go on. But you can't always do this without first lingering in the queasy muddle of your uncontrolled feelings.

We now know, through the work of pioneers in the field of death and dying, such as Elisabeth Kubler-Ross, that grief is not an event but a process that includes a myriad of emotions. These feelings may include shock, denial, disbelief, and anger, as well as longing, sadness, fear, disorientation, guilt, and depression. Any or all of these reactions are normal, although they do not occur in the same way with everyone.

Sometimes people who are familiar with the literature available on the grieving process think they're supposed to go through set stages of grief in an orderly way—for example, shock, followed by anger, followed by depression, and so on. "Why am I so angry?" a perplexed woman once asked me. "I had my anger two months ago." I couldn't help smiling, because there is nothing rigid or predictable about grief. Although there is a process, it often has many loops and turns, depending on the circumstances of the people involved. Rarely does grieving follow a rational pattern.

If you expect to feel and behave a certain way about your parent's death, you may find yourself utterly confused and disheartened when anger or depression are experienced months after you have achieved what you believe to be a point of acceptance. I find that those who continue to suffer and those who have the greatest pain for an unusually long period of time usually do so because they were unable to express the full range of their feelings—acceptable and unacceptable—in the beginning. Those feelings may fester and start hurting later on. That's why I spend so much time in the early sessions of my group letting people talk about what they are experiencing. There, in the safety of that room, it begins to come out: the shock and denial, disbelief, anger, guilt, and depression. More will surface as times goes on, although some of it will be hard to reach.

It is understandable that shock and denial follow sudden, unexpected death. There is a small corner in the mind of every distraught mourner that hopes against hope for a reversal of reality—for the curtain to be pulled back and the dead parent to step forward, beaming, "It was all a big mistake!"

I also know that shock and denial are not just present when the death was unexpected. Although sudden death seems more unfair, and violent death seems more tragic, each death is shocking in its own way. A woman in one of my groups related how she felt deep denial, even though her father was eighty-six and his death followed a long illness. She told of clinging to her memories of him and searching for signs that he was really still with her. She said he appeared almost nightly in her dreams—dreams so detailed that she came to believe he "crossed over the void of death" to speak with her as she slept. She also told of walking down the street and seeing the back of her father's head only to discover on closer inspection that it wasn't her father at all. "I look for him in the museums we used to visit together before he became ill," she said. "Or in the park where he used to feed the birds. I pray that he will appear to me and give me a sign. I keep hoping one day to open my eyes and find him sitting in his favorite chair."

I asked her, "What would you say to him?" My question momentarily broke the spell of her daydream, then she began to sob. "I'd say how glad I was he was back!" she cried.

It is not unusual to have vivid dreams of the person who has died, and these dreams can be infused with meaning. Two years after her father died, a woman told me about a dream she had that was so powerful she could not stop thinking about it for weeks. "In the dream, my father and I were walking down a long tunnel. And there was a little girl with us; he was holding her hand. We walked for a long time, and at some point, my father and the little girl got ahead of me. I ran to catch up with them and came to a huge spiderweb. I could see my father and the little girl on the other side, but I couldn't get through. He was calling me, 'Come on, Ellen, just walk through it,' but I couldn't. Finally, he reached a hand through the web to help me, and I woke up."

I asked Ellen what she thought the dream meant. She said normally she didn't think very much about the meaning of her dreams, but in this case, it seemed very clear to her. "The web was the barrier between life and death; my father had crossed it, but I had not. The little girl was me as a child; she was also dead, because now I was an adult, my daddy was gone, and I couldn't be his little girl anymore. I wonder if I had stayed in the dream and taken his hand if I would have died. By waking up at that moment, I think I was choosing to live. No just live, but really have a life."

In Ellen's case, the dream had the effect of jolting her

out of her denial. It served as a moment of reckoning that enabled her to accept the fact that her father was dead and, more important, to decide she could choose to live without him. Now she was ready to do the work.

Some people stay in denial for a long time, which is a warning sign that something is very wrong. Recently, a woman came to see me in my office. In appearance, she was a highly functional person. She was well-dressed and articulate, and she told me about her responsible job with a large brokerage firm. You'd never know she was having a problem until she began to describe her living situation. Her mother had died two and a half years ago, and now she was living with her father in her parents' house. She described in great detail how she kept all of her mother's things exactly as they were the day she died: "Her makeup, lotions, and perfume bottles cover the dresser. Her toothbrush and shampoo are on the bathroom shelf, just as she left them. Her clothes are neatly folded in the bureau and hanging in the closet. My father keeps saying we should pack everything up, but everytime he suggests it, I go crazy. I won't let him touch a thing, and we have frequent arguments about it."

I asked her when she planned to put her mother's things away, and she said she wasn't sure. "She might be angry," she explained.

In a very gentle tone, I said, "Do you think your mother is going to come back?"

She didn't answer, and I asked again. "Do you think your mother will need her things when she comes back?"

Finally, she said, "I don't know." Of course, she knew intellectually, but she wasn't emotionally ready to give her mother up.

This woman needed greater help than most people to

resolve her denial. She was in a state of complicated grief reaction. More often, the feelings of shock and disbelief fade as the mind adjusts to the permanence of the loss. But the emotional anguish doesn't end there. In the months after the death, shock is often replaced by an all-consuming anger at everyone, including the parent who died. People have said to me:

- "I'm so angry at the hospital personnel. They were completely cold and clinical. My dad shouldn't have had to die in that horrible place."
- "Why didn't the doctor try to save him? Isn't that what doctors are for? We had faith in him, and he let us down. You should have seen the bill! I hope the doctor dies as miserable a death as my father."
- "I'm furious with my mother's family. They were so insensitive at the funeral. They kept saying, 'It's better like this.' Better for who? Couldn't they see how much I was hurting? Didn't they care that she was gone?"
- "My father promised me that all his affairs were in order, but after he died, we discovered they weren't. Between the lawyer and the taxes, we were almost wiped out. My mother is one step away from being homeless. How could he leave us such a mess to deal with?"
- "I can't get over my anger that even when she was sick, my mother kept smoking. She couldn't take a puff of a cigarette without coughing up blood. Didn't she realize she was killing herself? Didn't she care what it would do to me to lose her? No. She only cared about what she wanted. She was so selfish. I don't think I can ever forgive her for killing herself and leaving me alone."
- "My sister didn't shed one tear at the funeral, and she flew home the day after. I had to take care of everything

myself. I'm furious with her, and I still can't stand to talk to her."

A woman whose mother died after years of health problems stemming from diabetes told me how angry she was with her mother. "She should have been more careful," she exclaimed. "For years I told her she had to pay attention to her diet, be sure to take her medicine. She was like an incorrigible child. She never listened to me. She mocked death. Well, who's laughing now? Not me!"

A man told me about his elderly father, who had had arthritis in his knee for years. "Suddenly, at age eighty, he decided to have knee replacement surgery, and he didn't even consult me. I would have talked him out of it; he didn't need to be having unnecessary operations at his age. After the knee surgery, he went downhill. He had a blood disease and it developed into cancer. I'm so mad at him that he went ahead with that stupid operation. The operation was a success, but the patient died."

Sometimes anger can provide the fuel that keeps you going in the difficult days after your parent dies. But eventually, the anger fades and then depression may set in like an icy reality. Every morning you wake up with the blank awareness: "He's dead . . . She's gone." The people around you are back to business as usual, and you feel empty, lonely, and sorry for yourself. Sometimes you adjust to it and it begins to feel all right—or at least not too bad. You normalize the less-than-functional state. But for some people it's paralyzing.

It is common at this point to have little interest in the very things that once gave you great pleasure or satisfaction. "I have always loved my work," said a buyer for a women's boutique. "But after mother died, I lost all interest. Just like that, I didn't want to do it anymore."

At this point, it can seem as though the sad feelings will never go away. Depression is like being in a room with no exit. But even this debilitating grief doesn't have to make you a victim. I know it may feel as though you are out at sea on a life raft and can't do anything but flail around and drift where it takes you. But even in times of deep powerlessness and uncertainty, you can assert some control. Stop looking at mourning as a state of helplessness; begin to see it as a job. Remind yourself that taking an action usually makes you feel better.

I like the way David A. Crenshaw, a clinical psychiatrist specializing in grief counseling, describes the process in his book *Bereavement*. Dr. Crenshaw outlines what he calls the seven tasks of mourning. I have elaborated on this insight to describe what those tasks may be for you.

1. *Acknowledge the reality of loss:* Accept that your parent has died and a reunion is impossible. His or her everyday presence and influence can no longer be a part of your life. It may seem cruel. You may object and say, "My mother will always be a part of me," and, of course, she will. But her influence is now an abstract rather than a concrete reality.

2. *Identify and express the emotions of grief:* There is a function to grief. It forces you to stop what you're doing and pay attention. Let yourself experience your pain and don't repress it. People have said to me, "I'm afraid if I start crying, I'll never stop." Or, "If I let myself really feel the pain, I might die." Trust that you will stop crying eventually. It is often said that you won't let yourself know

or feel something until you are ready and are sure you can tolerate it.

You may think the depth of your feeling is beyond what it should be. You may say to yourself, "Get a grip. It's over." But the reality of the death doesn't sink in, because what you're experiencing is emotional, not rational.

3. *Commemorate the loss:* Find ways to create rituals that honor the memory of your parent or parents. This doesn't mean you should build a shrine. But rituals, especially the familiar ones of religious tradition, can be comforting and releasing. For example, in the Jewish religion, a memorial candle (the Yahrzeit candle) is lit on the anniversary of a family member's death. In the Catholic Church, you can arrange to have a Mass said in your parent's name. The Jewish religion also has a custom of naming new babies in honor of a dead relative. Your rituals may also be tied to family traditions, or you may invent them now.

4. *Acknowledge ambivalence:* Accept the fact that your relationship with your parent was complex—as all important relationships are. Don't expect to resolve these feelings and put them away in a tidy pile. Take them out and examine them. Often, people who have the most conflict with their parents when they're alive have the hardest time when they die. There are so many loose ends—so many thoughts: "If only I had another year," or "If my father were alive, I'd know the perfect thing to say to him"—as though a resolution could happen by magic. The implication is that you're sure your parents would respond now just the way you've always wanted them to; given the chance, you could miraculously know the "right" thing to say.

Your ambivalence might be related to the death itself. Maybe you're relieved to see a long, harrowing illness come to an end. If you were the caretaker of an elderly, sick parent, the death may release you from a terrible burden. The internal conflict between mourning and relief can drive you crazy with guilt and confusion. Actually, it's perfectly understandable and acceptable to feel this way. The question is: Can you let these feelings of sadness and relief coexist?

5. *Accept ambivalence:* Begin to come to terms with your parent and your relationship with that parent as it really was. You can resolve a conflict without your parent being there, because what you really want to say is something to yourself, not to the other person—especially since you can't orchestrate what that person will say. So, tell yourself the truth: "My mother was sometimes unfair." Or "My father was overly critical." You can find resolution by acknowledging the way things were, and by accepting responsibility for the choices you made.

6. *Let go:* Say good-bye to your parent in a manner that allows you relief from and acceptance of your loss. You may do this by packing up the parent's things or distributing them to others, or by disposing of a parent's ashes in a meaningful way. Maybe saying good-bye means going to the grave site and talking out loud to your parent, writing your feelings down in a journal, writing the parent a letter, or commemorating the death in a special way.

7. *Move on:* Eventually, you adjust to the environment that no longer includes your parent, and you begin to redirect your emotional investment to the people and circumstances of your life.

A parent's death forces you to take a fresh look, to ask yourself, "Is this who I really am? Is this what I really want?" It's natural to reevaluate your life after an encounter with mortality.

You may be relieved to know there is a road to travel, that many people have traveled it before you, and they have left markers along the way to guide you. When you're overwhelmed with shock ("I can't believe it!"), or anger ("It's so unfair"), or depression (I can't go on"), it helps to trust that you may come to a point in the road, as so many others have, where you say, "I realize I haven't thought about Dad for an hour." And then, "It doesn't hurt as much every day." And finally, "I can live with this loss."

I have an important caveat to offer about the process of grieving. Although there is a wide range of normal emotions associated with the death of a parent, some reactions may be warning signals that you're in trouble and need additional outside help. If you're not sure, ask yourself these questions:

• Are you still unable to believe that your parent is dead, even after a protracted period? Do you hope for and expect your parent to return? Do you believe, deep down, if you wait long enough or do certain things, your parent might come back? Look to your actions for clues. For instance, if you haven't moved any of your parent's things after a lengthy period, that might indicate your unwillingness to accept the permanence of the loss. Watch your feet, not your mouth.

• Have you cut yourself off from friends and family and isolated yourself for what feels like an unusually long time? Do you have no interest in seeing them, or feel no concern for what is happening in their lives?

• Are there things that used to give you pleasure that

no longer do? Have you noticed this lack of interest has gone on for a very long time?

• Are you unable to take care of your basic needs—such as eating, paying the bills, cleaning your house, putting gas in the car?

• Has there been a marked deterioration in your health? Have you experienced a dramatic change in sleep patterns, notable mood changes, or severe appetite changes?

• Are you dependent on alcohol or drugs? Do you use alcohol or drugs to numb the pain of your loss?

• Are you worried about yourself, or do people who care about you express concerns that are chronic and specific?

• Do you have thoughts of suicide? Do you think about hurting yourself?

If you answer yes to any of these questions, don't assume you'll get better all by yourself. You may be embarrassed to admit, even to a therapist, that your life has become so unmanageable. But I urge you to set aside your embarrassment and find the help you need. If you're the kind of person who has always been in control and that's the way others perceive you, it may be especially difficult. A woman once told her family doctor she was worried about how poorly she was coping, and he responded, "Not you!" He was professionally trained to recognize distress signals, but even he failed to do so. The point is, you may know in your heart if you need help, and you can choose to get it whether others believe you need it or not. If you do nothing, things will not get better.

CHAPTER FIVE

DISCOVERING WHERE TO DIG

*Unless we remember
we cannot understand.*
—Edward M. Forster

"I don't have any recent pictures of my father displayed in my home," Irene admits to the group. "They're all at least forty years old. My favorite is a photograph of the two of us that was taken at my wedding. He's so handsome in that picture. It's the way I like to remember him—tall, ramrod straight, wavy dark hair, a brilliant smile." Her face glows, and for an instant it's possible to see the young bride behind the lines of age. She continues, "The old man I took care of, with no teeth and gnarled, arthritic hands, the one who didn't always know what day it was . . . that wasn't my father. Anyway, not the father I remember."

Tonight's session is about memories. I've asked each person to bring one to share, but it's time to do a little digging into what these memories can reveal. Sometimes they're sweet and happy memories, like Irene's. Other times, they indicate distortions. Most people have a great investment in remembering things a certain way—even if the memories don't reflect reality.

I tell the group about a woman who came to one of my workshops. "She only had negative things to say about her relationship with her mother: They were always fighting, her mother couldn't stand her—on and on. Then she brought a picture to class. It showed her and her mother standing together, arms around each other. The look on her mother's face was so filled with affection for her daughter, I was astonished. I asked the woman, 'Did you pay her to look this way?' She was taken aback by my question, but it was so stunningly clear that the stories she had told did not fit the photograph she chose to show us.

"When people remember the past, they tend to generalize: 'We always fought,' or 'We always laughed,' or whatever. These overall perceptions get solidified, but when a specific memory conflicts with them, it challenges you to consider what was real.

"Our sharing tonight is designed to open those doors. It's up to you to do the looking. Does anyone else have a memory to share?"

Arlene speaks: "My fondest memory is the night Daddy took me to a Leonard Bernstein concert. I was twelve years old, and it was the first time he ever took me out alone. I wore a beautiful dress and my mother put my hair up. She even let me wear her favorite earrings. I remember that we went to dinner first, to a nice restaurant. I felt like I was on a date. He made me laugh, and the concert was . . . well, we both loved music and it was spectacular. Daddy was a gorgeous man, very regal, and I was so proud to be seen with him. I will never forget that evening."

"Your mother and brother stayed home?"

"Of course. My parents were so different, I'm amazed they ever got married. My mother didn't have much use for classical music; her idea of a good time was to watch a baseball game on TV. She and my brother were like peas in a pod. They did their thing and Daddy and I did ours. I never could understand why they were together. He was much more refined than she was . . . had much better taste. And she never appreciated his musical genius."

"It sounds like you idolized your father, but had problems relating to your mother," I say.

"We were so different; we couldn't communicate at all. She once accused me of looking at things through rose-colored glasses—that was just before she left him. She told me things were more complicated than I could understand, that it had been hard for her trying to scrape by and put food on the table while Daddy pursued his dreams."

"What was your reaction?"

"Well, I was very loyal to him. And I decided it wasn't my problem. They had their own relationship and it was their business. My relationship with Daddy was perfect."

"As compared with your relationship with your mother, which fell short?" I ask.

"That's right."

"Hmmm," I muse, "I wonder what it feels like to have a perfect relationship. I'm not sure I've ever met anyone who did. Perhaps you could explain."

"Are you being sarcastic?" Arlene asks suspiciously.

"A little." I smile to break the tension. "It's just something for you to consider. *Perfect* is a big word to use when describing a relationship. Some people would say it's an oxymoron."

"I sure would!" Eileen exclaims, and everyone laughs.

"Well," I conclude, "I always like to think of family relationships as being precious, not perfect. You might consider how hard you had to work to maintain that perfection. Anyone else?"

"My memory is of my tenth birthday," Richard says. "My father and I didn't do things together very often. But he took the day off from work and we went fishing. I had never seen that side of him—warm and relaxed, like a regular dad. Or, at least, what I thought a regular dad was supposed to be like. He was usually such a busy, intense person. It was a nice change. I even have a picture from that trip, and this week I dug it out and put it on my desk."

"Did you go fishing other times after that?" I ask.

He thought for a moment. "I'm not sure . . . maybe once or twice. Isn't it funny that I can't remember?

"Why do you think you chose that memory?"

"I know my father loved me and my brother, but he was very busy. He worked a lot, and he didn't have much time for us when we were kids. He wouldn't get home until eight or so, and we usually didn't have dinner with him. My tenth birthday is a sweet memory for me, because he took time off just to spend the day with me."

"That's why my fondest memories are of the holidays," Patricia says. "It was a real family time. My mother has never been an especially good cook, but we always did the complete Jewish ritual, and our house was full of family and friends and people who didn't have any place of their own to spend the holidays. I particularly loved Rosh Hashanah, the Jewish New Year. It was the only time Papa ever became emotional. It was bittersweet, because he always named all of the people in the family who had died, and then he'd lead us all in reciting the kaddish, the prayer for the dead. But mainly I remember that there was so much happiness in the room, such a feeling of family and belonging."

"You told us your father was a Holocaust survivor. Was he able to tell you what that meant to him?" I ask.

"Somewhat. Both of his parents and his only brother died in concentration camps. Their pictures were in scrapbooks in our home, but my father rarely talked about them. He wasn't a very communicative man, and my sisters and I didn't ask a lot of questions. We were raised to believe that the most important thing was to be normal American girls. Most of my friends never even knew I was born in Israel. Sometimes I was embarrassed that my parents didn't speak perfect English. I'm ashamed of that feeling now. But during the holidays, none of those bad feelings were there. I felt close to them and to my heritage. Now, I cherish those memories because we'll never have times like that again."

"The Jewish holidays this year must have been very difficult for you," I say.

Patricia's eyes tear. "Everything was different. My mother did her part with the food and preparation, and we all chipped in. But the first night of Rosh Hashanah, with my mother's brother sitting at the head of the table where my father always sat, it was—" she breaks into tears and can't go on.

"Holidays can be the worst time," I say sympathetically. "We invest a lot in holidays; they often comprise our favorite memories from childhood. Many things change when a parent dies, but often it's the holidays that most graphically reveal the loss. With Thanksgiving, Hanukkah, and Christmas coming up, that's probably on everyone's minds."

"We've been through two Christmases now since my father died," Helen says. "Our family seems like it's shrunk so much with his death. He was only one person, but he was quite a person! Last Christmas, we visited my husband's parents in Florida, and it was the worst Christmas of my life. It was seventy-eight degrees on Christmas Day! That's not the way it's supposed to be."

"Our family seems shrunk, too," Patricia says, dabbing at her eyes. "Before Papa died, it never struck me how few people there were left—how much the Holocaust took from us. All Papa's family—people we never knew."

Everyone is silent. The conversation about the holidays and Patricia's moving reflection on the personal cost of the Holocaust has struck a nerve. Often, people don't know what to say during these moments. I let the silence be until someone else is ready to talk.

Finally, Eileen speaks. "Am I the only one who doesn't have happy memories?" she asks bitterly. "If I were to take a snapshot of my childhood, it would be of three scared kids cowering in the corner while my dad ranted and raved, hoping we wouldn't get hit. My mother did what she could, but she was no match for him. I never understood why she didn't leave him. He was a drunk. He hurt us. I know she must have been scared for us."

"Did you ever ask her?" I question.

"I tried to once. It was a long time after Dad went into a program and stopped drinking. All of us kids were adults by then. Her attitude was, why bring up negative memories from the past? It's over now. In my family, I was seen as a troublemaker because I couldn't just say OK, it's in the past. Let's forget it."

"Sort of like having an elephant in the room and everyone stands around saying, 'What elephant?' " I comment.

She smiles in spite of herself. "That's my family."

"Did you ever confront your father directly?"

She shakes her head. "That's the funny thing. I regret it now. I've often played the tape over in my head of what I'd like to say to him. But while he was still alive, I . . . I don't know, I guess I felt intimidated. Now, however, I want to bring it all out of the closet."

"I gather your brother and sister feel differently about that."

"It's something I've never been able to understand," Eileen says. "They were there. They experienced the same abuse I did. But now they're so willing to just let it go, even though obviously both of them have scars. My sister has been married twice, both times to alcoholics. What does that tell you? And my brother gets more and more like my father every day. I don't think he hits his kids, but I know he drinks too much. They're both in deep denial."

"Can you let that be?" I ask. "Not to say their choices are OK, but can you accept that they've chosen differently from you?"

"But don't they need to face it?"

"It may be that you're the last person on earth they can hear that from," I tell her. "You can't be their conscience. Don't give them something to fight with you about."

Eileen looks doubtful. "I'll have to think about it, but I'm angry."

"So, why are you here?" Matt asks bluntly. "It sounds like you didn't care if your parents lived or died, so I don't understand why you're having such a problem."

Eileen begins to respond angrily, and I cut in. "Matt, what makes you so angry about what Eileen is saying? Chances are, she's touching something in you."

"Look," he holds up a hand defensively, "I understand not everyone had the kind of wonderful relationship I was able to have with my mother. I don't blame you, Eileen. I'm sorry for your problems. It just doesn't seem to be the reason we're here."

I try again. "Matt, you think she's different from you, so she shouldn't be here. But why should it matter to you? Can't she be here for her own reasons—even if they're different from yours?"

He shrugs.

"I thought we weren't going to judge," Marian says. Everyone is so surprised to hear her speak, they swing their heads around to stare. She blushes and wiggles her leg. "I mean, I think everyone has their own problems."

"Well put, Marian," I say. "Actually, there's more ambivalence in this room than you think. Remember, relationships are complex. Our purpose is not to cover your parents in glory or turn them in their deaths into what they never were while they lived. It's to gather information and learn important things about your relationships with them that will help you function better in your present life."

Everyone seems to be paying attention, although I suppose I sound like a broken record. It's important to keep reinforcing. I look around the circle. "Anyone else?"

"When I was thinking about this exercise, a whole series of thoughts popped into my mind," says Mary Ann. "It surprised me that I would remember this particular incident. As I've said before, my mother was wonderful. She was my role model and we absolutely adored each other.

I usually deferred to her because—well, I don't exactly know why. I suppose because it pleased her. Also, I trusted her opinion on most things. Anyway, my memory is of going to a furrier with her about five years ago. She was buying me a coat as a birthday gift. She fell in love with this one coat, but I really didn't care for it at all. We went back and forth about the coat, and she was quite insistent. I became angry with her, which was rare for me, and yelled at her right in the middle of that very fancy store." She grimaces at the memory. "It was so out of character. I shouted, 'Who do you think you are? I don't want it!' "

I raise my eyebrows. This is a new side of Mary Ann. "How did she react?"

"She was furious, and rightly so. She told me I was being ungrateful, which was true. You would have thought by her reaction that we were on *Candid Camera* and the whole nation was watching instead of just a couple of bored salespeople. I got the coat, but she was still disgusted with me for days."

"How do you think your mother would explain your behavior?" I ask.

"She would say I was trying to hurt her," Mary Ann replies promptly.

"Were you?"

"Of course not, although I could understand her thinking it. I embarrassed her, and she was trying to be nice to me."

I press on. "Do you wish you could redo that moment?"

"Yes. It hurt her and I never wanted to hurt her. It wasn't typical. I adored my mother and she adored me."

"Enough to let you have an opinion?" I ask.

Her face clouds. "I'm not sure what you mean."

I try to explain, choosing my words carefully. This is

touchy ground. "Sometimes when parents say, 'I just want you to be happy,' the parenthesis is, 'As long as it's the way I think you should be.' I remember one woman who used to say her father would do anything except let her do something he didn't want her to do. There's a subtle message that your judgment is being questioned, but it's a disguised message."

"I can see that," Mary Ann says. "I'm just not sure it describes my mother."

"I mention it because so far, the only two stories you've told us have to do with your not doing something she wanted and her getting angry. I'm just offering it for your consideration. There may be a different explanation altogether."

Matt breaks in again, his voice heated. "You seem to be encouraging us to think of negative things to say about our parents," he says accusingly. "Is that what this is all about? I'm really uncomfortable with this kind of talk. It seems like you badger people until they admit something was wrong with their parents. Sure, everyone has faults, but why shouldn't we remember the positive things? You make it seem like there's something wrong with that."

"It's not my intention," I say calmly. "This conversation isn't about negatives or positives or whether your parents were good or bad. It's about considering possibilities— things that might contradict hard and fast beliefs. Your parents weren't one-dimensional cardboard cutouts. They were flesh-and-blood human beings. As I have said many times, the best way to pay tribute to your parents is to remember them as they were, not as you wished them to be. Sometimes those memories aren't pure and idealized; they're gritty and real. Sometimes we think our parents weren't capable of being selfish or needy—in the same way that we and all other human beings are sometimes selfish and needy. I don't consider that as being negative. It's a way of taking an honest look at a portrait of life as we have all experienced it. It's how things really are. Mary Ann, the questions you may need to ask about your relationship with your mother are: How much choice did I have? Did I have a hard time saying no? Were the decisions really mine? Were my options restricted?"

"That rings a bell with me," Jane says. "When I was young, my mother and I had a relationship that was different from the kind any of my friends had with their mothers. I started thinking about it this week when I was concentrating on remembering. My memory is of my mother and me sitting outside on the patio and her telling me that my father was a brute. I was maybe thirteen years old. My parents had a somewhat rocky relationship. They loved each other, but they argued about everything, and my mother considered me her ally. We often had these 'just girls' sessions when she would talk about their relationship in the most intimate details. A lot of it I didn't really understand, but that never stopped her. I don't think she was a very stable person. Looking back, I realize it was very important to her that I take her side. . . . " Jane's voice trails off and she seems wistful. "She was my mother, but she wanted us to be more like friends."

"Did you ever wish your mother wouldn't tell you those things?" I ask.

"I don't know if I could have put it into words. I remember my girlfriends always used to be jealous of me because I had such a neat mother. They loved to come to my house for sleep-overs because my mother was just like one of the girls. At the time, it was great. I was really popular. But maybe my mom was the popular one. I don't know. As I grew older, her behavior started to make me uneasy. I thought that sometimes she used me to make herself feel better. Everything was about her, not me. I guess I wanted it to be about me sometimes."

"So you wanted her to be your mother, and she wanted you to be her friend?"

"I don't know. I didn't know how to be her friend. She wanted me to take her side against my father, but sometimes I didn't even understand what he did that was so bad."

"Tell me," I say to Jane, "was there ever a time when you didn't take her side—when you took his side?"

"No." Then she remembers. "Oh, yes, there was this one time."

"What happened?"

"I don't even remember what this particular argument was about," Jane says wearily. "Something stupid, probably. I think I piped up and said, 'You know, maybe Dad has a point,' or some comment like that. My mother stared at me with her eyes popping out. She couldn't believe it. Then she huffed off. For two weeks, she barely spoke to me, like I was the grand traitor. I remember feeling awful."

"That was your punishment for taking his side?"

"I never did it again. As I got older, I stayed out of their arguments altogether. I never really got to know my dad. My mother was such a dominating force."

"It sounds like she wouldn't let your father be your father," I say. "He was always her husband and that was the only way it was safe for you to relate to him. Does that sound right?"

"Yeah." She looks sad. "I think it's been helpful for me to remember this and talk about it. But I'll tell you one thing, I'd take my parents back in a minute, fights and all, if I had the chance. In a way, this realization makes me feel closer to my mother—more sympathetic to her. She was a very unhappy woman. I feel sad for her that she had no one but me to confide in. I think she must have been very lonely. I'm not making excuses for her. I just think I understand her better."

An hour and a half has passed almost before we know it. The air seems heavy with the weight of memories. Each person is lost in a private revery—the relating of memories driving others to the surface. Before they leave, I ask them to do another assignment for the next session. "It might help to alleviate some of your confusion to consider how your parent or parents actually viewed you—what they would say about you, not necessarily in public, but if they were being completely honest. I want you to make a list of the words your parent would use to describe you. Use simple one-word descriptions. Bring your lists next week and we'll look at them together."

As the group breaks up and I am preparing to leave, Helen comes up to me. "I realized something tonight," she says eagerly.

"What's that?"

"All this time, I thought I was really here because of my father, but when we were talking about memories, my mother's face kept showing up. You know, she died when I was a teenager."

"Yes, I remember."

"I've thought of her over the years, but her face has grown so remote I can hardly recall it. I thought my deepest feelings, the ones that brought me here, were about my father. But now, her face is popping into my head. I can't stop thinking about her. Last week I went back and got out some of the old picture albums. There was one picture when I was maybe two. I was sitting on her lap. She was wearing a big, oversized sunbonnet and laughing. Suddenly I missed her so much."

"It's like the experience of someone touching that tender spot and it hurting all over again," I remind her.

She seems awed. "That's right. I didn't think of it that way. This is all so unexpected. It's confusing, but also a little bit like a gift. I thought I had forgotten my mother, and now I have her back. This is good, really. Thanks." She gives my arm a squeeze and hurries out the door.

I feel good as I start to straighten up the room. Moments like that are always welcome. I also feel hopeful about the events of the evening, although I know at least several people are feeling the pain of their discoveries. We have moved quickly from the experience of immediate grief to something deeper. The memories have released a new dynamic in the room. Whether the participants have fully recognized it or not, some advances have been made in the discovery process. But while I've been through it many times before with many other groups, it doesn't prevent me from having moments of worry. I trust the structure of my work and know what I am doing is designed to help, but I also know I can't really control how individuals choose to relate to their discoveries. I find myself thinking about Matt. He is very resistant to digging, and I know the resistance will act to protect him from seeing things. He'll defend himself against change. I can plant a seed which may or may not grow. I hope he's listening. He doesn't have to agree to hear what's being said.

I leave the room and walk out into the cool night air, but I don't leave the group behind. I know from experience that I carry a bit of everyone around with me.

The one-word lists are hard for everyone. During the week, I receive two phone calls. One is from Patricia, who tells me she doesn't want to do the exercise at all; it's too frustrating, she says, because her father didn't use descriptive words. The other is from Richard, who says he can only think of one word to put on his list, "and it's not a very creative one." I reassure them both and encourage them to do their best.

The group straggles into the next session clutching scraps of paper, notebooks, and three-by-five cards. The mood has shifted somewhat, and I know why. We have moved away from revealing random feelings and are starting to do more specific and rigorous work.

When everyone has pulled their chairs into the semicircle, I begin with a few words of explanation. "I know you're curious about these lists," I say. "Some of you have already mentioned that they're hard to do. Their purpose is to explore how things were perceived in your families—where credit was given. What do I mean by credit? Simply put, different families place different value on people being artistic or good sportsmen, or having advanced degrees or being well-dressed or looking a certain way, or being sociable, and so on. Credit can be given or denied for the same trait. For example, your family might admire your generosity with them, but criticize you for buying gifts for friends. Your lists will reveal something about where credit was placed in your family. Let's go around the circle and read what you've written." I turn to Mary Ann, who is seated to my right, and motion for her to begin.

"I wrote, *patient, loyal, feminine, quiet.*" She stops. "Is that the kind of thing you're looking for?"

I nod and repeat, "*Quiet.* Say more about *quiet.*"

"For the most part, when I wasn't yelling at her in

furriers, my mother thought of me as being a quiet woman. She often said so."

"And she valued that?"

"It just was. I deferred to her—that's why I put *loyal* on my list. I trusted her opinions."

"And you rarely challenged them?"

"I think it was her way of taking care of me. It usually didn't occur to me to challenge them."

"OK. Amanda?"

Amanda reads: "*Loving daughter, hard worker, single, single, single.*" She rolls her eyes as she repeats *single,* bringing a laugh from the others, which loosens the tension a little.

"So, your mother would describe you as single," I say with a straight face.

"Well, I *am* single."

"You've told us before that this was a big worry of your mother's," I say. "Do you think she worried about it more than you did?"

"Hmmm . . ." she thinks it over. "I'd like to be married, but I have to say it was a bigger problem with her than it has been with me. I've always tried to think of myself as complete and capable on my own. My mother was from a different generation."

"OK. Helen?"

"My father thought I was very special," Helen says slowly, "so I put *special* on the list. We were on our own after my mother died, except for his sister. But to tell you the truth, I'm not sure what else. Maybe he was proud of me. He was happy when I married Harry. He always said I made a good choice."

"Did he ever directly tell you how he felt about you?"

She looks shocked. "No . . . I guess not. He wasn't very good at expressing his feelings."

"It's a man thing," Amanda assures her, and the three men in the room look briefly chagrined while the women chuckle knowingly. I move on. "Irene?"

"In recent years, my father would definitely describe me as nurse, maid, cook, and bottle washer," she says. "But I also wrote on my list, *stable* and *responsible*."

"Were these qualities that were valued in your family?" I ask.

"Well, my father valued them because they were the opposite of what my mother was," Irene reveals. "She let herself go, she was obese, and she didn't take care of her diabetes. That's why she died at such a young age. I think he appreciated the fact that I didn't inherit those traits from her."

"And your brother?"

"Tom has always been a steady, responsible man," she says. "But he has told me in the past that I should lighten up. If you were going to ask what he values, I'd have to say it's his baseball card collection and his golf buddies."

"You sound like you think you and your brother are quite a bit different, as were you and your mother."

"I'd have to say yes," she answers readily. "My father and I were the most alike."

I glance around the circle. "Isn't it fascinating what these word lists reveal? Matt?"

Matt pulls out a sheet of paper and reads, "*Rock of Gibraltar*—that's something my mother actually said, so I put it on my list. Also, *reliable, intelligent*—don't laugh—*handsome*."

"Was being handsome important in your family?" I ask.

Matt is surprised. "Why did you pick that one to comment on? I don't think my mother really cared, it was just something she thought. Being reliable and intelligent were two things she cared about."

"What did your brother get credit for?" I ask.

"That's a good question," he answers grudgingly. "Mother seemed to think he was fine, even after he abused her. She was his mother, so she was blind to his faults."

"And to yours as well?"

"My mother was a very generous woman," Matt explains. "She tried to see the good side of everyone. It wasn't always so wise, because some people will take advantage if you're too nice."

"Are you talking about your mother or about yourself?" I ask kindly.

He stares at me blankly, but I suspect I've hit home. He has also revealed an important piece of information. His mother was never estranged from his brother. I wonder about those last two years after she had left Matt's brother's house to live with him. What had transpired during that time? I'm aware of how sensitive Matt is to these issues. But for now, I move on. I say to Patricia, "It's your turn."

Her face is flushed. "I had so much trouble with this assignment, you wouldn't believe it. It was like Papa and I had an unspoken love—we cherished each other. But he was a man of few words. I did realize, though, that one thing he valued about me was my interest in our religion. I was the one he discussed religious subjects with. He also thought I was a good mother. I know that. Sorry, I didn't do so well."

"You did what you could do," I say. "Remember, no grades. Arlene?"

She reads: *"Musically talented, companion, soul mate, beautiful."* She stops to explain, "He always said I was beautiful. Once I threatened to cut my hair, and he almost died. Of course," she adds dismissively, "my mother was a very beautiful woman, but that wasn't enough. Daddy treasured intellectual and creative companionship. She couldn't provide that."

"So, when you say *musically talented,* you think that's a compliment coming from your father, but it wouldn't necessarily get you credit with your mother?" I ask, suspecting the answer, but wanting her to see it.

"No, my mother wouldn't think that."

"OK. Richard?"

"I had trouble, too," he admits. "I would love to write *good lawyer,* because my father would have valued that. Unfortunately, he died when I was just getting started, so he never had a chance to see me in action. One day, I would have liked him to call me *colleague.*"

It's a touching comment. I think of the pride involved in having one's beloved parent present one with such a compliment. "Anything else?"

"That's it for now. Sorry."

"No sorrys, please. Jane?"

"This is a list for my mother," she says. "*Friend, confidant, ally.* Also, *responsible,* because I'm a nurse. And, of course, *single,* although, unlike your mom, Amanda, mine thought that was a compliment. Oh, and *plain.* She thought I was plain. I'm having a hard time with how my father would describe me. I'll have to think about it more."

"I'll bet your mother didn't really think you were plain," Barry says.

"Did you know her mother?" I ask.

He smiles guiltily. "Oops. I know, I know. I'm 'fixing.' "

"Good for you that you see it!" I grin. "Eileen?"

"As far as I know, my father didn't ever think about

me as a person," she replies. "But my list for my mother is easy: *Difficult, caustic, loud mouth, troublemaker.*" She grimaces. "A lovely picture, huh?"

"I think I can tell by your tone that these weren't the ways people got credit in your family," I say.

"No kidding."

"All your words are so angry," Irene says in her best mothering voice. "I'm sure your mother must have loved you."

"When did you meet Eileen's mother?" I ask.

Irene laughs and says, "Well, I bet she loved her."

"How would you know?" Eileen asks tersely. "It's what I wrote, OK? I'm the one who knows."

Irene pulls back in her chair and says defensively, "I just think no family is all bad."

I hold up a hand. "See how easy it is to 'make nice'? We're not dealing with objective realities with these lists. They're about how families give credit and perceive one another. So, Barry, it doesn't matter if you think Jane's mother thought she was plain or not; or Irene, whether you think Eileen's parents felt a certain way. I'm sure you can see this is not real information. You didn't know them so how can you say? Maybe it makes some of you uncomfortable to listen to someone say things that sound negative or hurtful. But how can you possibly know they are wrong? Maybe it comforts you. But it closes the door on their feelings. Where do they go after you challenge them, except to get defensive? Neither of you learn from that kind of interaction. Does that make sense?" Barry and Irene nod.

Eileen says, "I want to explain one thing, if I may. I do think my mother loved me. My list describes how she felt about me when I started trying to get some resolution in my family. I'm still trying."

"I know. It's one of the reasons you're here," I tell her. "Marian? Do you have a list?"

"Yes." She straightens up on her chair and unfolds a sheet of paper. "My mother would say nice things about me, I think. I wrote: *Good student, funny*—I used to crack her up with my jokes." She stops to compose herself as tears begin to spill. "*Sloppy dresser*—that she didn't like. And *beauty queen*." She laughs through her tears. "I know that's what she'd say. Of course, she hasn't seen my latest haircut."

We laugh. Marian's hair is cut so close it's almost nonexistent.

"So," I say, wanting to get Marian talking, "where was the credit? Was being a good student important in your family?"

"It was the number-one thing," she answers. "My mother was a hound dog when it came to studying. And I wasn't always such a good student when I was in high school. My parents tended to hold up my brother Jack as an example, which I didn't appreciate too much. But I got my act together. As far as being funny, that's another big one. Everyone was a joker. If you didn't have a snappy comeback, forget it."

"So, being smart and funny were the values. Is your father smart and funny?"

She dips her head to examine her feet. "He's smart. He's a scientist, so I guess that makes him smart. But funny? No, you wouldn't call him funny."

"Would he think saying someone was funny was a compliment?"

"Wow!" Marian blinks her eyes. "You ask so many questions!"

"I know. With me, it's genetic."

"My father doesn't necessarily think being funny is so great," she answers. "But he doesn't mind it, as long as you're successful in other ways."

"That's interesting. It's always so amazing how different families are constructed. Don't you think so?"

Marian glances at me shyly. "Uh-huh."

I turn to Barry. "You're the last. What do you have?"

Barry reads, "*Baby of the family*—that's embarrassing. Um . . . *intelligent, entertaining, secretive, broke*—I never had any money. Still don't." He grins charmingly.

"I gather 'baby of the family' is a label you've heard a lot, I say. "You've mentioned it a couple of times before."

"Yeah, they all think of me that way," he says. "It embarrasses me now, because obviously I'm not a baby. But my parents and sisters have always kind of taken care of me, and that's been nice."

"How about *secretive?* Why do you think your father thought you were secretive?"

"Uh . . . well, sometimes, even though we talked a lot, there was something there between us."

"Did your father ever mention it?"

"Not directly. But he always asked lots of questions, and sometimes he wasn't very satisfied with my answers. I tended to walk on the surface—make jokes instead of revealing myself. It's something I've learned about myself recently," he says quietly.

Barry has not told the group he is gay, and of course, it's his choice to do so or not. I am naturally curious about whether or not he will. But now our time is up so I don't press him any further.

"What do you think about this exercise?" I ask the group.

"Intense!" replies Richard.

"I agree," says Jane. "Something that struck me when I tried to do this exercise was that I didn't know what my father thought of me. I couldn't do a list for him! My mind went blank. I remembered that when I used to call and he answered the phone, he'd never stop to chat. He'd immediately say, 'Hi, honey, here's your mother,' and hand the phone over to her. It never occurred to him that I might want to talk to him, and it never occurred to me that he might want to talk to me."

When we end that night, various people stop and chat with one another, almost reluctant to leave the safe place this room has become. I realize they are getting more than they bargained for. Perhaps they're learning that safe and comforting doesn't always mean unchallenging. This is very challenging work we're doing, as detectives of the most complex mystery of all.

CHAPTER SIX

A SHAKEUP IN FAMILY SYSTEMS

*Death ends a life, but it does not end a relationship,
which struggles on in the survivor's mind toward
some resolution, some clear meaning, which
it may never find.*
—Robert Anderson

Being a family member is usually not simple; families, like life, are very complex. Usually things are contained within a system, in which each person plays a lifelong and established role. The death of a parent can shake up that system, and the result is often chaotic and unpleasant. A man in my group once referred to the loss of his father as "opening a can of worms." At other times, the hole left by the person who died is filled very quickly and everyone pretends there's no longer an empty space.

When a death occurs, there's no escaping its impact on all of the other relationships. The death upsets the balance. It reveals flaws and weaknesses that were covered up for a long time. The death of a parent can bring into sharp relief the myths, fears, and struggles within each family. But it can also present an opportunity to reshape the system, create new closeness among the members, and resolve old differences.

Every family lives by myths, which are a loose collection of stories, attitudes, and labels. I like to think of it as "family folklore." This folklore is reflected in the labels that are often given and the distortions that exist in defining the roles different members play. For instance, people might say, "My mother was a saint and my father was a bum," not realizing that their mother and father worked together in an established pattern. Maybe he was the one who expressed the hostility for both, while she remained silent. Or maybe a woman who spends extravagantly does so because she knows her husband is frugal. People often say things about couples like, "How can she be with him? She's so nice and he's so rude." It may seem inexplicable from the outside, but on the inside, it may work perfectly. It's like driving a car. You have the gas pedal and the brake and both play opposite yet synchronized roles.

I am not suggesting a theory of opposite attraction, nor am I saying that couples always have such differing traits. I am only using this example to show how what is true about family systems is often not apparent, and that even people who appear to be victims are often full participants in the dynamic.

Each child has a special designated role in the family. It isn't overtly talked about, but the roles exist: For example, one child might be the responsible one—a role often assigned to the eldest. Another might be the "baby," another the quiet one. One might be the mediator, another the jokester.

This dynamic might be easier for you to understand with a little background about the concept of family systems.

Families take a long time to create the systems they live by. Anyone who has tried to change a family system—by creating new rules, or suggesting new attitudes or behaviors—can attest to the power of its entrenched rules and boundaries. Often the people who challenge are labeled "black sheep" or are considered sick or crazy—depending on how important it is for the rest of the members to maintain the myth.

The continuum within families can go from one extreme to the other, from no rules to a rigid game plan. But even in families that seem to operate in an "anything goes" mode, there are assumptions and understandings. As a youngster once put it so well when asked what the rules were in his family, "Oh, we don't have any rules, but you better not break them!" At a young age, most children have already absorbed the important information about their family's rules and boundaries. They may not be able to articulate it directly, but if you ask a child how many times he has to ask his mother for a cookie before she says yes, he'll immediately tell you, "Five." He already knows that four times is too few, and she'll relent before six. He'll also know exactly when to ask. Just when his mother gets home from work, when she's frazzled or tired. Children have impeccable timing. They also figure out very early which parent plays certain roles in the household: Mom will make them do an hour of homework; Dad is good for a little extra money, and so on.

Limits and consequences are easily absorbed and used— as anyone who works with teenagers will tell you. I have listened to teenagers calculate the known consequences of what they want to do and make their decisions this way: "If I come home late, my dad will get really upset and he'll yell at me for about fifteen minutes. That's definitely worth it to go to the party!"

When people in my group start talking about members of their families, they fall into the comfortable scripts, developed over many years, of speaking of parents, brothers, and sisters as known quantities. They can easily describe a family gathering right down to who says what and who does what. These patterns have been a long time in the making. They're reflected in statements like, "That's just like my sister."

The death of a parent is a great shock to the family system. The balance is shifted. It affects everything. I once had a woman in my group who described the way it was before her mother died. Her husband's parents lived upstairs and her mother lived across town. Whenever she and her husband would have a fight, he'd storm upstairs to his parents' apartment, and she'd go to the phone and call her mother. That was their pattern for years. After her mother died, he still went upstairs when they fought, but she had no one to call. The balance was off. Her anxiety was great when she cried, "How are we going to have fights now?"

Especially in the early period after a parent dies, family members may react stridently toward one another in the confusion. Under stress, people tend to revert to intuitive ways of behaving. Old patterns, laid aside—like alcohol abuse and overeating—can reemerge.

Human beings are imperfect, and so too are families. Relationships among siblings include jealousies, resentments, and a whole collection of emotional time bombs. With a parent's death, these bombs might explode in accusations or hurt feelings.

Families can also respond by pulling together more tightly. A woman once recalled gratefully that she rediscovered her sister after her parents died. A young man recalled how the older brother he always thought disliked him turned into a friend during the week they cleared out their mother's house together. The possibility of change and transformation always exists, no matter how tight the family system is.

But more often, it is the spilled hurts that produce the most vivid encounters after a parent dies:

- "You were always the favorite!"
- "You were so selfish. Couldn't you even have remembered to send a card on his birthday?"
- "You broke Mom's heart!"
- "You could do no wrong where she was concerned. But I'm the one who got stuck with all the work!"

On and on it goes. Favorite child, misfit, outcast, controller—the roles play out, contorted and enlarged by the power of death.

There's a great deal of feeling attached to these roles. And even after a parent is no longer living, the competition can be fierce to be the best, most loving, the one who suffers the greatest grief. People who come to my groups or undertake counseling with me often say they feel shut off from or misunderstood by their siblings. There is a tendency to judge brothers and sisters harshly—especially the way they behaved in the period around the parent's death. I often hear comments like:

- "My sister didn't shed one tear during the funeral. She was like ice. I couldn't understand it. Didn't she love our mother?"
- "My brother got drunk the night our father died, and said some pretty ugly things about Dad. He had me in tears. How could he do that?"
- "We both got the call that my father had died at the

same time, but it took my sister four hours to get to the hospital. My mother and I had to wait forever for her to show up. What could have been more important that it took her so long?"

• "After the cremation of my mother's body, my sister took the ashes home with her. It was never discussed. She just took them. Now she says she doesn't know where they are. She doesn't know where my mother's ashes are! I can't even talk to her anymore. I'm furious!"

When I ask the people who have complaints like these how their siblings would see things, they rarely have an answer. Often, it hasn't occurred to them that different members of the same family may have very individual ways of expressing their grief: The stoic who can't cry; the drinker who escapes from his pain into alcohol; the fearful soul who cannot bring himself to visit a dying parent in the hospital; these responses are all more complex than they might seem. How easily we jump to conclusions about the motivations of others and fail to appreciate the underlying emotions. I saw this clearly with the man who told me this story about his father's death:

"I was there in the hospital with my mother and sisters when he died. They were all wailing; at one point, my mother literally threw herself on top of his body, clutching at him and screaming gibberish. I just stood there, in a corner of the room, watching them. My feelings were very powerful, but I knew I had to remain in control. I had been a Marine combat officer during Vietnam, and I'd seen a lot of death. I had trained myself to remain calm. My eyes were dry. I stayed that way all during the funeral—which, of course, I was in charge of arranging since I was the only one who wasn't hysterical. I remember standing at my father's grave like a stone statue, while around me everyone was sobbing and carrying on. That night, back at the house, one of my sisters came up to me and said with such disgust, 'You're so cool, you make me sick. Don't you feel anything?' I turned and walked out of the house. I was deeply hurt. She knew me . . . how could she think that?"

When a parent dies, the adult children can be forced to confront the truth about family relationships. Any ambivalence you may have felt toward one another is brought to the fore, and a lifetime of hidden resentments and regrets are ripped open to create fresh wounds. There is often the fallout of a lifetime of words spoken and left unspoken.

In other cases, there may be a continuation of normal patterns, except they may grow more intractable. One of the children—the one who was the most sensitive to the parent—may carry the banner for the others, becoming the stand-in for the parent's values.

The child who tries to build a shrine to the parent might be offended when others in the family want to tear that shrine down. The sibling who insists that the best way to cope is to accept the loss and just move on might be confronted angrily by the one who wants to hold fast to grief.

Even though children might have grown up in the same household, their memories of that experience may be quite different. It is not unusual for siblings to see the same behavior, but from a different lens. One of the most graphic examples of that is the "rag doll story." The rag doll story was told to me by a woman as indicative of her father's wonderful qualities. When she was a small girl, about six, her family took a vacation trip to visit relatives; it was a two-day drive, and they spent one night each way in a motel. Since there were eight children, the trip was a pretty massive undertaking. This woman remembers only one detail from the trip. On the day they started home, they drove for two and a half hours before stopping at a motel. There she discovered that her favorite rag doll had been left behind, and she started to cry inconsolably. Her father, she told me, was so considerate of the trauma involved in not having her precious doll, that he jumped into the car and drove all the way back—a five-hour round-trip—to get the doll. The moment remained in her memory forever as the most wonderful thing her father had ever done. But while she was telling her side of this touching little tale, my mind was filling with the broader implications of the events she described. I imagined her mother, exhausted, with eight mouths to feed and put to bed, alone in a motel while her husband went off on a five-hour excursion. I imagined her siblings and how they must have felt. I said to her bluntly, "This is a cherished memory for you. Do you think it's a cherished memory for your brothers and sisters? Your mother?" She was flabbergasted. In all those years, it had never occurred to her how they might have felt about their father driving off into the night to chase her rag doll.

Another woman told of how her maternal grandmother had written her memoirs before she died. They were in longhand on lined paper, the sheets tied together with big ribbons, and the stories covered her whole life. The woman was most fascinated with reading the stories about her mother and aunt during their childhood, the grandmother describing a happy, carefree pair who had many adventures and much fun. When her aunt read the memoirs, tears came to her eyes. She said her mother had captured perfectly the spirit of their youth. However, when her own mother read the memoirs, her reaction was different. She was furious. "These are all lies!" she yelled. "Things weren't so rosy."

The woman who told me this story was absolutely fascinated by her mother's reaction; she'd had no reason to believe the stories were anything but true, especially after her aunt's corroboration. But when her mother calmed down she explained to her, "My mother and sister could never stand the idea of anything being upsetting, so they created a world where nobody was ever upset. We weren't allowed to express negative feelings, but believe me, there was plenty of silent tension."

I hear stories like this frequently. Occasionally, I've had two siblings in my group at the same time, and I marvel at the difference in their perceptions. If you didn't know they were related, you'd think they grew up in different families. I remember in particular the two sisters who each had a different impression of the other's relationship with their "difficult" mother.

"You always stood up to her," one of the woman told the other.

"Stood up to her?" she responded in shock. "How can you say that? I totally avoided her. You're the one who stood up to her."

The other woman shook her head vehemently. "No, I always cowered in her presence. I never told her about anything I did that I thought she wouldn't like."

I suppose it's not surprising that siblings would see things differently. So much of what we internalize depends on who is doing the speaking and who is doing the listening. I find that if siblings can allow one another to hold on to their own "truth," they can become close and allow for the others' experiences. Otherwise, there are battles to show who is "right," and the winner takes away an empty victory.

I'm not trying to suggest that there are always conflicts. Some siblings get along very well, but if tensions in the family are high for other reasons, the death of a parent tends to exacerbate the problem.

Although some families work out very sensible caretaking arrangements for elderly or sick parents, existing rivalries may be intensified when one sibling has been the primary caretaker for a sick or aging parent before death. "My brother lived a thousand miles away, and he flew in to see our mother maybe twice a year," one woman recalled bitterly. "Meanwhile, I was there in the same city, visiting her every day, taking her shopping, being attentive to her needs. When she got sick, I moved her into my house with me, and did everything I could to make her comfortable until the day she died. I never voiced one word of complaint. She had been a wonderful mother to me, and I owed her this. But even so, I did sometimes think my brother should be doing more. My husband agreed; he thought my brother was a bum. When our mother finally died, I handled all of the arrangements. I bought the burial plot, went to the funeral home and chose the casket, made all the calls—obituaries, family, friends—and even chose the dress our mother would be buried in. My brother and his family flew in for the funeral and he acted grief-stricken. But his show of grief left a cold feeling in my heart because, although I knew he loved our mother and felt sad, I also knew that her death wouldn't disrupt his life for very long. He'd go back home and carry on unchanged, while I lived with the loss and took care of all the details. I spent months in my mother's house sorting through everything. It never occurred to my brother that maybe he could help me; he certainly never offered."

This woman's greatest moment of pain came while she

was packing up her mother's things and making arrangements to sell her house. "It was a terribly emotional experience. Each room held so many memories. I went at it slowly, doing a little every day. I saved her bedroom for the last, and I'll never forget that day. I was cleaning out her dresser, and I discovered that one of the larger drawers was crammed with cards and notes from my brother. I swear, every birthday, Mother's Day, and Christmas card he'd ever sent her was in that drawer. She'd saved them all. Some of them were actually quite funny, and one Mother's Day card was especially humorous. It read: 'You've been like a mother to me.' That was my brother! But nowhere in the house did I find a similar drawer with my cards. She hadn't saved them, just my brother's. That hurt me more than I can say—and how I wish I had never found that damn drawer! It changed my memories of her forever. I proved my love to her every day, while my brother barely lifted a finger. But he was the one she loved best. His cards were precious to her. I guess mine weren't. What more could I have done?"

An interesting footnote to this story shows how different people's perceptions can be. When I told this story years later to one of my groups, a woman interpreted it this way: The mother saved his cards because she needed them as a reminder of him, while the daughter was present every day.

When there are tensions among siblings about the care of aging parents, it can help put things in perspective when they evaluate how decisions in the family get made. For example, the woman embittered because the entire care for her mother fell on her shoulders might ask herself: How did this come to be? Did my mother ask me to be the one? Did my siblings ask me? Was it just assumed? Did

I volunteer? Did I feel I had no choice? Did I honestly believe only I knew the right way to take care? And so on. Events and decisions don't just happen; they grow from the way in which families are structured, the roles people are expected to play, and what is assumed and expressed within the family.

Fights often break out over the disposal of property and possessions, and even the most mundane events can seriously increase the tension among siblings. For the most part, the bickering is not caused by greed, but by the attributes and meanings given to the possessions: Who was loved more, who did more, who will be in charge, who did Mom want to give her ring to? Remember, everyone is trying on their new roles for size, and it can leave siblings fighting for elbow room.

Many parents fail to make clear how they want their goods disposed of, or don't leave wills, and this is also revealing, especially if the parent was quite elderly or had been sick for a long time. Was it an oversight? Fear of facing death? Something else? The siblings and surviving spouse are left to mop up the mess. One woman complained that she and her three brothers and sisters had been left as coexecutors of their father's estate, an arrangement obviously headed for trouble. "It's a nightmare," she told me. "We've never agreed on anything in our lives and we can't agree now. I'm so mad at them, I could spit!"

"You're angry at *them?*" I asked in surprise. "What about your father? He's the one who left this mess."

I wasn't trying to be brutal, although my remark seemed harsh. It was the truth. Surely their father had been aware of the dynamics among them. Could he not have foreseen that they would be unable to handle this collaborative effort?

Again, when it comes to the disposal of goods, the sibling who did the most when the parent was alive will often feel that he or she is owed a bigger piece of the pie.

One fifty-two-year-old woman who had nursed her widowed father through his final years when he was deteriorating and suffering from Alzheimer's recalled how indignant she was the day she and her sister went through his house and discussed the disposal of his property. "She was acting like this should be a fifty-fifty deal, but it didn't seem that way to me at all. I was the one who had cared for our father—which wasn't easy, believe me!—and paid all of his bills for years. I felt I was entitled to more than half."

She said she felt terrible for saying it, and admitted that no such agreement had ever been made. "In fact, my father's will, which was written before he got sick, divided everything in half. But was that fair? I didn't think so. I would have expected my sister to offer me first choice of everything. Instead, she made a big stink about taking my father's war medals, which I would have liked to have had for sentimental reasons. I gave up and let her have them. God, that irked me! Ever since then, there has been a real distance between us."

One young man told me that he had always had terrible clashes with his mother. "Obviously, my older brother was her favorite. My mother was very conscious of style and appearance, and my brother had the right look and attitude. I was different—overweight all my life, clumsy, an indifferent dresser. She reminded me constantly that I never measured up. You have to understand, my mother's family was very 'high society,' and there was always a lot of money. I think her attitude toward me was, 'You can dress him up, but I still don't want to be seen with him.' In the weeks that my mother lay dying, she had the best care money could buy, but I felt I should be there. I moved into the house, sat by her bed, helped the nurses try to feed her. Not my brother, the beloved one. He stayed in Texas until two days before she died. Then he came for the death watch, and he brought his wife, who was a real bitch. During that time, he seemed impatient for it to be all over, and his wife actually had the nerve to start going through my mother's closets looking for clothes and furs she'd like to take. I was horrified, and I demanded that she stop. My brother and I really went nose to nose on this, but it didn't matter. It was all just awful.

"Anyway, my mother died the next morning about four. The nurse got me up and told me. I was really very upset. I woke my brother and he hardly reacted at all. He refused to go in to see her. We had the funeral three days later, and they flew back to Texas that same night—after taking whatever valuable items they could get their hands on. They didn't even pack the suitcases themselves; they had the housekeeper do it. That was cold! I vividly remember that the night after they left, I went into my mother's room and sat at the window staring out at the stars. It was a crisp, clear evening. I started talking to her out loud: 'I love you. I hope you're all right wherever you are. I promise you I'll miss you even if he doesn't.' In the end, I was the one who showed her love and devotion, even though she had such a hard time loving me."

This man and his brother went on to engage in a lengthy legal battle over their mother's estate. They were both very wealthy, and their mother's will left each a generous inheritance. But this battle wasn't about money. It was about the emotional legacy each had been left to deal with—the son who didn't have to work hard to be accepted and the one who couldn't get accepted no matter what he did.

Because a parent's death seems like a great injustice, there is also the tendency to look around for someone to blame. That "someone" might be the brother or sister who took charge of things as the parent's life ebbed. Now the second-guessing begins:

• "Why did you insist the doctors give Dad more sedatives? He was completely out of it for weeks. He was hardly breathing. I think it hastened his death."

• "Where did you *find* that doctor? I thought you said he was the best. You don't know anything, do you?"

• "How dare you make the decision to turn off the life support systems! I know we put you in charge, but I never expected that you'd decide to play God."

• "That nurse you hired didn't give a damn. She should have been paying attention every minute. She spent more time sitting in the kitchen drinking coffee and doing crossword puzzles than taking care of her patient. I'd like you to explain why she wasn't even in the room when Mom stopped breathing."

The unspoken message: "I want to make it someone's fault." The person who is on the receiving end of such vitriolic remarks often sees things differently.

One woman angrily remembered how her sister, who had stayed totally uninvolved during their mother's long illness—who, in fact, had begged her sister to take care of things because she just couldn't handle it—said later, to a mutual friend, "I should have paid more attention to my mother's care. Maybe things would have been different if I'd been involved."

"Of course, it got back to me that she had said that, and I was furious and hurt. She didn't want anything to do with our mother's care, and now she was blaming me for not doing enough. How dare she!" she cried indignantly, remembering the final weeks of her mother's life. "The truth is, she couldn't stand to be around Mother. Those final weeks were horrible. She was constantly vomiting black and green bile, and the smell was unbelievable. No one wants to see or remember their mother like that. It was humiliating for her and ugly for me, but you do what you have to do. Obviously, I was stronger than my sister, so I forced myself to deal with it. I kept thinking, 'This is my mother. I have to do it.' Anyway, she has a lot of nerve to criticize me now. Before she starts judging me, she should look at her own behavior."

In the early stages of grief, stories of rage against siblings pour out of people in this way, the fallout of fear, sadness, confusion and, in some cases, the accumulation of years of unresolved issues. People's memories crystallize as they try to deal with their loss, and even the small slights from long ago start to fester. Suddenly, a man is angry that his brother got to sit up front with their parents on car trips, or that his sister always got the drumstick at Thanksgiving. Favoritism, punishment, and privilege all spring to life from long-distant recollections. Sometimes the fury can be like a dam breaking, and it leads to surprisingly positive results. A woman described the family's first Thanksgiving dinner after her mother died: "My sister decided to make the turkey dressing different that year. After forty years of my mother making it the same way, she decided to change the recipe. I blew up at her and threw a pan against the wall. I knew my anger was way out of proportion to the incident, but I couldn't help it. She screamed back and dumped the dressing in the trash. Then we both stopped and saw ourselves and started to laugh hysterically, then to cry. It was such a relief."

The reconfiguration of the family puzzle is different when there is a surviving parent. Here, too, children often have trouble adjusting. Maybe the parent is not responding to the loss the way you would expect or want. Suddenly, you can't communicate. You seem to be grieving for two different people—and in a sense you are. Children often fail to consider that although they have lost a parent, their mother or father has lost a spouse. Their relationship with the deceased was entirely different, and their reaction to the death may not be comprehensible to you. I've spoken to widows, for example, who told me what they'd never dare to tell their own children—that they were relieved by a husband's death, especially when it followed a long, debilitating illness.

Surviving parents might also seem remote to their children, because they are dealing with levels of pain and longing that are far different from theirs. Often widows and widowers will say with frustration, "My children have no idea what I am feeling. They expect me to take care of them, to make their sadness go away. When I can't be there for them, they accuse me of being cold or of not being a good parent. They just don't understand."

If the surviving parent is elderly, ill, or infirm, there are additional pressures on the children. "The whole time my mother was dying, one thought kept burning in the back of my mind: What are we going to do with Dad?" a woman admitted. "I hate to say this, but it would have been easier if he had died first. He was very old and forgetful; I knew he couldn't live alone. I had visions of him leaving the oven on and setting fire to the house, or falling down in the shower. But could I stand to put him in a home? Bring him to live with me? I was so consumed with worry about my father, I never had time to grieve for my mother."

Then again, the issue with the surviving parent may be that he or she is *not* helpless. If you're still having trouble accepting the loss, it can be bruising to see the other parent go on with his or her life. Perhaps you think the parent should be with you and maybe take over the role your other parent played. For example, a man who always received money from his mother was angry when his father refused to continue the financial support after she had died.

One woman marveled at the change in her mother a year after her father's death—a change that made her uncomfortable. "My mother was like a different person," she said. "Happier, more self-confident. I have to admit I was uneasy. I wanted her to be happy—it isn't that. But you have to understand that I had never known her as anyone but my father's wife. That was her identity. Now, here she was, going out on her own, meeting people—she even took a cruise. She was enjoying life, and deep down I saw it as a betrayal."

"You wanted her to sit home and grieve for your father?" I asked her.

"No!" she insisted, then shrugged. "Maybe. I don't know. I missed him so much, and she was like the keeper of the flame. If she went on and made a life of her own, even got remarried, who would sustain his memory?"

Another woman was very hurt when her widowed father married a woman twenty years younger. "Was he glad my mother died?" she wondered. "It didn't take him long to find a replacement."

I asked her if she had shared her feelings with her father

and she said no. "He has a new family now. He doesn't care what I think."

"What do you think he would do if he *did* care what you think?" I asked.

The question stopped her cold. She had no answer. In that moment, she realized her father's remarriage was not a sign of his lack of regard for her. Once she acknowledged that, she could go on to explore her own mixed feelings about her mother's death, the expectations she had of her father, and the fear she would no longer play an important role in his life.

A seventy-year-old man put things in a different perspective for me. His wife had died five years ago, and he had moved to an apartment, started doing volunteer work in the community, and was considering remarriage. "I had my darling wife for forty-some years," he said. "Every day with her was a blessing. My kids can't understand how I could get married again. But we old codgers know something they don't know: Life is terminal, and you've got to live it while you can. Maybe the old rules and proprieties don't matter as much when you're seventy as they do when you're forty because you see that life is going to end one way or another."

Over time, feelings can either go underground or be addressed openly, or families can become more entrenched in their positions. There are always choices. And even in families where the priority is to return things to "normal" as soon as they can, it is an unmistakable fact that things in the family will never again be the same. The roles shift, just as sand shifts to fill an empty place in the desert.

The fallout isn't necessarily negative. The death of a parent can also bring about positive changes in relationships or draw family members closer. Suddenly, people are confronted with how fragile life is, how easily the people they love can be taken from them. They may try harder to build bridges, respect the others' individuality, and create opportunities to be together as a family.

Much of what occurs in the shifting family dynamics depends on the history of communications in the family. As Murray Bowen, a pioneer in the field of family systems wrote in *Living Beyond Loss,* all families have either an "open" or a "closed" relationship system. In an open system, the family members are free to communicate their most important inner thoughts and feelings to others. In a closed system, there is an automatic reflex to protect oneself from anxiety by avoiding taboo subjects. These taboos can be anything; it depends on the individual family. But typically, death is a big taboo subject. Bowen notes that any change—and especially the death of a central family member, like a parent—is going to upset the emotional equilibrium of the family. But it will be much harder for everyone to adjust if there is a closed system.

If your family operates in a closed relationship system, the best thing you can do is to begin asking questions. As Monica McGoldrick, an expert in family loss, writes:

> Questions are the most powerful tool for gaining a new understanding of a family. Are dates of death barely remembered or honored as holy rites? How comfortable are family members in talking about the deceased and the circumstances of the death? Are both positive and negative memories available? The more information family members have, the more perspective they will gain on themselves and their lives and the better chance they will have to face the future with openness.

CHAPTER SEVEN

OPENING A FAMILY DIALOGUE

*Family life is too intimate to be preserved by the
spirit of justice. It can be sustained by
a spirit of love which goes beyond justice.*
—Reinhold Niebuhr

In my early sessions with the group, it sometimes seems as though each individual is floating alone in space, wrapped in a very private pain. The people in the room may as well have been born without brothers or sisters, aunts, uncles, or cousins. Although I constantly ask them about the other people in their families, they are reluctant at first to bring them into the picture. They live in a narrow tunnel of grief, and the only other person they welcome inside that tunnel is the lost parent whose lifelong presence has now been removed.

But as we move on and dig into the complexities of the past, the relationships within the larger family—most particularly with siblings and the surviving parent—become the focal point of our discussion. I ask everyone in the group to close their eyes and imagine they are standing outside of a window, watching a scene set inside their childhood home. In this scene, they are observing a dinner table, with all of the members of their immediate family present. I ask them to look long and hard, and consider what they see. Who is seated at the table? Where are they seated? What is being said? What are the dynamics of interaction taking place among the people in the room?

"Now," I say, "walk around to another window that gives you a different view. What do you see now? Consider how your perspective is different. This is your family of origin—the only one you have," I say quietly. "Our purpose is not to change this family, but to see what you learn when you look at it from different angles. As you view the scene through the window of memory, you might feel strong emotions. Examine them as though they, too, were outside of you. Memories are flooding back of happy moments, laughter at shared jokes, arguments, tensions, the ebb and flow of family life. Observe it as it is, without making changes. Try a third window. What view does that give you? What did you not see, and why? Because it was hidden, or because you didn't look? There are facets of people that are ignored unless you use a wider lens."

This exercise is about observation, not change. Even so, I realize that what they are viewing is part reality and part myth. We have already explored some of the myths present in this group. For example, Arlene's pronouncement that she was her father's child and her brother was her mother's child; or Mary Ann's belief that she was the one among all her siblings who really loved her mother; or Matt's belief that he is the one true son. These and other myths colorize the view inside the family. But tonight we'll try to rub off some of the coating and look deeper.

They sit with eyes closed in the quiet room as the minutes go by, overtaken by the spell of the past. Emotions flicker across their faces like photographs on a blank screen.

After a while, I tell them to come back to the present, and they open their eyes—some reluctantly, I can tell—blinking and rubbing them as though they've just come awake and are disoriented to be once again sitting under the bright classroom lights. "Now," I say, "let's talk about these families of yours."

When we reach the point in our sessions when we extend the conversation to encompass the rest of the family, it is often very difficult. Several people in the group have already admitted to feeling angry at or distant from their brothers and sisters or their surviving parent. I acknowledge their reluctance to probe into family relationships, saying, "Some of you have told me that you'd prefer not to spend time discussing your siblings, because you don't think they play a relevant role in your recovery. Maybe you have strong feelings of alienation or anger, or are simply not close. But remember the total picture of your family—the one you have just viewed through the window—and know that the relationship you had with your deceased parent did not exist in a vacuum. All the other participants had a role to play, too.

"Let's begin by talking about how the various members of your family have dealt with this loss. For example, how did they react to the death? Who was there at the time and who wasn't? Did you talk to one another about it? Who took care of all the practical details—calling people, arranging for the funeral, burial, cremation, and so on? Were there any disagreements that occurred around the death?"

"None of us were there," Marian says sadly, "because it was an accident. My brother Jack took care of everything, I guess. And my dad. We haven't talked about it since. There are no hard feelings or anything like that. It's just . . . it's hard in general."

"I think we have to acknowledge that your experience was different in that respect," I say to Marian. "A sudden, violent death, especially if the parent is relatively young, is going to take a different toll on the family members. You had no time to get used to the idea."

Barry recalls: "The night my father died, my mother, sisters, and I went straight from the hospital to my parents' house, and Mom took out an old bottle of brandy. None of us are very big drinkers, but we poured each person a drink and we sat around the kitchen table and talked for hours. I remember thinking how I didn't want to leave and go home, because then it would put a stamp of finality on my dad's death. We sat up half the night and I finally ended up crashing on the couch. I didn't want to leave."

"I took care of all the details," Patricia says. "No one else was even remotely capable of handling the funeral arrangements. I was exhausted by the time it was over. Then I had relatives and friends coming all week to sit shivah. I was so tired, I didn't even have time to feel sad. I mean, we were at my mother's house, but I was clearly the one in charge. But talk about it? No, not really. Except for my son. He was full of questions. It was interesting, really. Joel went through the funeral very well, and I was concerned about him because he was so young. Mama didn't think he should be there, but I felt it was an important lesson. Then, about a week later, he started getting up at night complaining that he couldn't sleep and was having nightmares. He wanted to crawl into bed with me and I don't usually let him, but I made an exception. I suspected all of this had something to do with Papa's death, but he wouldn't really talk about it. Finally, one day we were in the kitchen together. I was cooking dinner and he was playing at the table, and out of the blue he asked, 'What happens when a person dies?' I stopped what I was doing and sat down with him. I asked if he was wondering about Grandpa, and he said no, he was just wondering in general. Of course, I knew where this was coming from! I told him that some people believe that when you die you go to heaven and live happily forever, and other people believe that the dead person's spirit lives on in the world even after the body dies. I said different people believed different things. He was very interested in knowing if there was any proof. This was new territory for me, but I did the best I could. I turned the question around and asked him what he believed. He started telling me he thought there was a place everyone goes, but he wasn't sure, and he wanted to find out if there was any proof. He also said he was afraid if he went to sleep, he might die. It was an emotional conversation. I wanted to offer Joel comfort and protect him and assure him that everything was fine, but I didn't know how—and I couldn't lie." She stops talking suddenly and blushes. "I'm sorry. I didn't mean to go on like that."

"Not at all," I assure her. "This is important. People often don't realize that children are so observant of what's going on; they don't miss a thing. You can try to 'protect' them by refusing to answer their questions or, more commonly, by telling them lies meant to comfort. But it's more helpful to try to get them to talk about what they're feeling and what's going on in their minds.

"Children are affected by the death of a family member. They have feelings about it; they are curious. They have fears, especially if no one ever talks to them about death. To a child, the death of one person may indicate that their own death—or yours—is imminent."

"Do you think it was wrong of me to take Joel to the funeral?" Patricia wonders.

"Children absorb things whether you try to shield them or not. Truth is not necessarily dangerous for children; sometimes, it's hiding the truth that can leave them struggling. Then they have a sackful of questions nobody will answer. Patricia, a parent's judgment is the best guide for decisions about children. But it's my opinion that by age seven, children may attend a funeral, as long as care is taken to explain in advance what they will see."

"I agree," Richard says. "My brother and I weren't allowed to go to our grandmother's funeral, and we were ten and fifteen at the time. It was like, one day she was there baking cookies, and the next day she was gone. The euphemism was 'Grandma has taken a trip.' Of course, our response was, 'When will she be back?' " He laughs. "It was so silly. For a long time, we expected her to walk in the door with her suitcases and lots of presents."

"Death is in the closet for many families," I say. "But now there are several books that are very good, written for children. I'll give you the names later, if you like. But it isn't only children who are sheltered. A patient of mine whose mother had died told me how the family decided not to tell an elderly aunt who was living in a nursing home about the death. They thought if she knew her niece was dead, she'd have a heart attack. But after a few weeks, the aunt became quite distraught. She kept asking, 'Where's Phyllis? She hasn't called or visited. Where is she?' And then she decided, 'Oh, I must have done something to make her angry, because she never comes to visit me anymore.' She sunk into despair until they were finally forced to tell her. I think you can see how keeping the secret was doing more damage than telling the truth."

Irene is eager to speak. "Since our father's death, my brother and I have been avoiding each other—or it's more accurate to say he's been avoiding me. I've tried to figure out the reason, and I think it's because Dad's death frightened him so much. It must have been like looking in a mirror for him. They looked so much alike; maybe he saw a reflection of himself. You know, Orthodox Judaism requires that all the mirrors in a house be covered after someone has died, so you won't see the image of the deceased reflected in your face. That's Tom's fear. He hasn't aged very happily."

"How have you tried to reach out to him?"

"That's hard," she admits. "Now that we're both in our sixties—with me almost seventy—we're so set in our ways. When I talk to Tom, he seems cranky and distant, and he won't let me mention Dad. I don't want to push him— we're both too old to change now, and he's never been a very open man. But I'd like us to spend more time together, because we're all we have left. Besides, I get lonely sometimes. . . . "

"You haven't tried to tell him any of this?" I ask.

She shakes her head. "No, not yet. I've been looking for a way. The holidays are coming up. Maybe then. . . . " Her voice drifts off hopefully.

"Will your daughter be home for the holidays?" Patricia asks. "I don't know, maybe it will help break the ice. You can do things together with your daughter."

Irene lights up a little at the thought. "Yes, she'll be here. She and my brother always got along very well. As I recall, they used to play tennis together years ago."

"I notice this is the first time you've really mentioned your daughter, except in passing," I comment. "What was her relationship with your father like?"

"Well, she's in her forties." Irene seems to be searching for an answer. "I suppose they spent time together when she was younger. She hasn't lived here for more than twenty years. It's hard to know how she really felt about him."

"Was she at the funeral?"

"Oh, yes, she came and stayed with me for two weeks. I think it upset her, not so much because of Dad, but because she was worried about me. She's been making an effort ever since to stay in closer touch. In fact, it's unusual for her to visit during the holidays." She smiles wryly. "I raised her to be independent and that's what she is. I'm lucky if I see her every year or so. She's making an exception this year because of Dad's death, but I don't want to burden her too much. She has her own life."

"What do you think she would say if you told her how you were feeling and shared some of your fears and loneliness with her?"

"We've never had that kind of conversation before," she says doubtfully.

"Do you think it would make you feel better? Help her understand another side of you? Bring you closer?"

"Maybe. I don't want her to feel obligated."

I make a suggestion. "Irene, why don't you consider what makes you think sharing your feelings with someone who loves you is a burden. Sometimes strong, capable people inadvertently shut others out by not allowing them to help."

"I totally agree," says Marian vehemently. "My brother is twelve years older than me. Ever since our mother died, he's been acting like my parent. He feels it's his responsibility to shelter me. He's taken over all of my mom's business, and he won't tell me anything, even though I know there are problems. I want to scream at him."

"OK. What would you scream?" I ask.

"I'd scream, 'I'm an adult! I can handle it.' "

I laugh. "Imagine yourself screaming at him, throwing yourself to the floor, kicking your legs, and yelling like a child, 'I'm an adult!' " Everyone else, including Marian, laughs at the image.

"Well, maybe screaming isn't the right word," she giggles. "But you know what I mean."

Barry interjects, "I think I do. I'm older than you, but I grew up being the baby of the family, and that's the way I'm still treated. My mom and sisters have their whispering conversations, but no one tells me anything."

"Such as?" I ask.

"Oh, how Mom's feeling. Whether she has enough money. Any loose ends Dad may have left. That kind of thing."

"So," I address Marian and Barry, "what would you like to say to your relatives who are being overly protective?"

"I'd like to tell Jack that I really appreciate everything he's done for me, and thank him," Marian replies. "But then, I want to tell him to start leveling with me. We've never even talked about Mom. I haven't got a clue what he's feeling."

"I don't know what I'd say," Barry demurs. "I just want to be allowed into the grown-ups' club."

"This is an example of how benevolence doesn't always make people feel better," I note pointedly. "Irene, I think that's what I was trying to say about your wanting to protect your daughter. Sometimes people appreciate it more when they feel included. Marian and Barry, it sounds like you have pretty good relationships with your siblings. Why don't you try to tell them how you feel? Do you think you can?"

Barry shrugs, "I guess. Why not. I don't know if they'll listen, but it's worth a try."

"I can try talking to Jack," Marian says. "That is, if I can drag him away from the office for five minutes."

"Make a dinner date; get on his calendar. Remember, it's very hard to change family systems once they're in place. It might take many efforts. If you've always played a certain role or been seen a certain way, it gets cemented into place."

"Yes, like I've always been the one to take care of my parents," Amanda says.

"Right. Sometimes you have to force a change." I tell this story: "A woman in one of my groups was always overly responsible for her mother, who lived in another city. Every Christmas, she went home to be with her mother, and her brother never questioned that it was her role. Then, one year he called her up shortly before the holidays and said, 'I guess you're going home.' She replied, 'Nope, not this year.' He was flabbergasted. He said, 'What? You're going to leave Mom alone?' She said, 'I guess so.' What ended up happening was that the brother went home that year. What do you think would happen if you tried something similar?" I ask Amanda.

She seems very interested in the idea. "I don't know, but it sounds like something I should think over."

"When you choose not to play the role you've always played in the past, people can get angry or hurt. You have to know why you want to do something differently. It isn't easy," I warn her. I turn to Eileen. "Your hand was up. . . ."

"Yes, I have something to say about my brother and sister." She pushes stray blond curls out of her eyes. "I feel strongly that our family can't go on unless we deal with our childhood. Anyway, after we met last week, I decided it might help to get my thoughts down on paper, so I wrote this letter to Anne and Jerry—that's my brother and sister. I haven't sent it yet . . . can I read it?"

"Certainly." I motion her to go ahead.

> Dear Anne and Jerry,
> I don't really know where to begin, so I guess first I want you to know that I love you both very much.
> As I've told you before, I have been seeing a therapist for several years, trying to come to terms with the way things were when we were growing up.
> I know you don't want to remember how horrible it was for us, but I can't forget. Whenever I've tried to talk with you about this, you've just shut me out like it doesn't matter. When I was hospitalized after Mom's death, I know you thought I had gone off the deep end.
> The point is, we were all victims of abuse, not just me. You say it doesn't affect you, but Anne, you've been married twice and both your husbands were abusive; and Jerry, you obviously have a drinking problem. I think the problems we all have now are a direct result of what happened to us as kids.
> I don't think this is something we can put aside and forget. It haunts our lives now. We have to remember if we are to have any hope of not repeating the cycle.
> If you're willing, I'll meet you any time, any place to talk.
> Your loving sister, Eileen.

When she finishes reading the letter, Eileen looks at me expectantly.

"What's the likely response going to be to this letter?" I ask.

"I hope it makes them listen."

"Does it sound like what you usually say, or are you giving them new information?" I ask.

"I don't know what you mean?"

"It's been my experience that if you've already told someone something ninety-nine times, the one hundredth time you tell them doesn't usually change their mind."

"Oh . . . " She seems uncertain how to respond.

"Think about what you can say that's new," I suggest. "In particular, new information about yourself, not about them. However, in general, writing a letter can be a good way to diffuse some of the tension or anger you feel and allow you to speak more freely and honestly. Keep in mind you don't have any say in how they respond. Don't let this be another disappointment."

"I agree. Writing a letter was a real breakthrough for my sister and me—at least, I hope so," Mary Ann says. "This just happened in the past couple of weeks and I haven't mentioned it before because I didn't know what would happen."

It's delightful to hear Mary Ann talking in a positive way about someone besides her mother. I encourage her to go on.

She explains, "My mother was like the telephone operator in the family. She kept us all connected. She always knew what was going on with everyone. My sister and I got into the habit of letting Mother handle the communications, and we hardly ever spoke with each other directly. She'd call Mother and tell her what was going on, then Mother would pass on the news to me, and vice versa. It was the pattern. There was a distance between us that wasn't exactly uncomfortable—it was just there. I told myself it was because she lived in another city, but I think it was more than that. After Mother died, we started calling occasionally, but there was always a hesitation on the phone—like we didn't know what to say to each other. We both felt really—I don't know, awkward. A couple of weeks ago, I sat down and wrote to her. I said, 'I want to say something to you, and I don't know what. But I want you to know I'm thinking of you. If you don't know what to say back, that's OK . . . I love you.' I mailed the letter and I was very nervous, wondering what her response would be. A few days later, she called me at work, which in itself was a very unusual thing for her to do. She didn't mention the letter, although I'm sure she must have received it. She asked me for the address of a mutual friend, and then we talked for a while about other things and said good-bye. I felt wonderful after the call, even though we didn't say anything really significant."

"What do you think the call meant?" I ask.

"It was like my sister was telling me, 'I know what you mean, I don't know what to say either. But let's try to be closer.' "

"How do you feel about it?"

"Good. I don't know if it will lead anywhere, but we'll see."

I turn to Matt, who seems lost in his private thoughts. "Matt, you mentioned being quite angry with your brother. Have you spoken with him since the funeral?"

Matt shifts uneasily in his chair and stretches out his long legs. "You might say I've disowned him," he says. "Mother never would. She made excuses for him."

"You can't disown your own brother," Jane interrupts.

"Maybe not legally, but in every other way. He doesn't add anything to my life, I don't want to know him, I think he's a brutal man—should I go on?" Matt throws Jane a challenging look.

"You seem like a very lonely boy," Irene says compassionately. "Maybe it would help—"

Matt laughs sarcastically. "Obviously, you've never met my brother. Let's just drop it, OK?"

"It's a very big decision to disown your brother," I say to Matt. "Even though you feel estranged from him now, you are the only two people in the world who share certain memories. Here's an illustration. A woman in my group once talked about how she and her brother were so angry at each other that she didn't care if she ever spoke to him again. But over the weeks, as she considered it, she said she kept thinking about a scene from when she and her brother were little kids. They used to play together. He'd stand in front of a mirror and recite his acceptance speech as President of the United States. She'd stand on the bed in her nightgown conducting 'The Hallelujah Chorus.' What she said was, 'My brother and I are the only ones who had that experience. Even today, I can hum a few bars of "The Hallelujah Chorus" and we'll both crack up.' So, Matt, when you say you want to disown your brother, it's a major cutoff. It might be easier for you not to see him right now, but you can change your mind later. Your anger at him is like holding on to a hot coal. You're the one who is getting burned and can't let go. Do you see that as your only choice? Also, consider the timing and ask yourself whether you would have disowned him when your mother was still alive."

"I couldn't have. She still wanted him around."

"It's something to consider for your investigation," I say. "Now, let's move on and consider other changes in your family systems. A death in the family, especially the death of a parent, shifts the family system. Marian, you touched on that a little bit when you talked about how your brother has become parental. Has anyone else noticed that the roles in your family have shifted since your parent died?"

"I have an answer for that," says Mary Ann. "My mother was the focus of the family, in addition to being the telephone operator. Everything hinged on her; she organized all our family's get-togethers—not just for us, but for our aunts and uncles and cousins, too. When she died, I thought, oh, who's going to do that now? Being the eldest, I guess it naturally fell to me. For example, the holidays. My mother died in June, and since that time, her death has been the only thing on my mind. A couple of weeks ago, my brother called me and said, 'So, what are we going to do about Thanksgiving this year?' My first reaction was, 'Why are you asking me?' But then it hit me: I'm the matriarch now. So I'll be having the family—including aunts, uncles, the works—for Thanksgiving at my house, and trying to do everything the way my mother did it."

"How do you feel about taking on this role?" I ask her. "Do you feel forced into it, or are you glad to do it? Maybe a little of both—that's not unusual."

"I'm not sure yet," she replies candidly. "Let's see how Thanksgiving goes, then I'll tell you. Right now, all I feel is very, very busy. I'm not used to cooking for twenty-four people. I think maybe I like it, though. It's flattering."

"My brother is the executor of our parents' estate, such

as it is," Eileen says. "So, now he acts like he's the head of the family."

"What does he do?"

"He decides who gets what, who does what—you know."

"Did your parents leave a will?" I ask. "This is a common point of contention among siblings."

"Mostly, they left it to his discretion. It has led to some contention among us. I had a hard time getting Mother's ring, although it's no good to me, since it gives me a rash."

"Ah, yes." It was one of the first things Eileen mentioned earlier on.

Irene says sadly, "The problem is, my role didn't change. It disappeared."

"That's a change, isn't it?" I ask. "From caretaker to—what?"

"I'll have to think about it," she sighs.

"An odd thing has happened between my brother and me," Amanda says. "When my mother was alive, most of our conversations centered on him. She'd call me and say, 'I'm worried about your brother. He hasn't called lately.' Or 'Your brother is under a lot of stress right now.' No matter what we were talking about, she always brought the conversation back to him, even though he didn't seem to need so much worry directed his way. He had a wife and kids. It bugged me—made me feel like my life wasn't as important to her as his. Maybe she didn't think I needed her as much as he did. I don't know. Then, after she died, I found myself doing the same thing—worrying about my brother, calling him more often, offering to do things for him. I stepped right into her role."

"Do you think this would have pleased your mother?"

"Oh, definitely." Then she has a flash of insight. "Gee,

this sounds just like that old saying people have after someone dies: 'Your mother would have wanted it that way.' ''

I laugh. "That's a favorite. The question you might want
to ask is whether or not you think you have a choice. Is
taking care of your father and brother getting in the way
of other things you want to do?"

Amanda's voice is very serious now. "I've been thinking
about this a lot lately," she says. "I'm fifty years old and
I'd like to meet a man, but here I am, taking care of my
father and brother like some spinster sister from another
era. What's wrong with me?"

I don't respond, and she answers her own question. "I'm
beginning to realize that part of the reason I have trouble
meeting men is because of my family commitments. A
couple of weeks ago, I was out on a date—a rare occasion!—and after dinner, I had to find a phone so I could
call my dad. This guy couldn't believe it, and as I was
standing there at a pay phone listening to Dad go down
the usual list of everything he'd eaten that day, suddenly
I couldn't believe it either. Something's got to change. I'm
just not quite sure how to go about it yet."

The discussions we have in the group about family relationships always get tangled and frequently sidetracked. I
supposed that's appropriate when you consider that families themselves are like mazes, with many twists and turns.
But as I leave the group and begin walking home, I reflect
that we have turned a corner and made progress. I don't
mean that in any defined way. This is not a scripted play
where the scenes follow neatly to a grand and healing
conclusion. But I have trained myself to recognize the
barely visible signs of movement within a group. For example, I'm not sure whether anyone noticed it, but tonight

we hardly spoke of the dead parents at all; our emphasis was on the living. I am also impressed by how serious this group is about probing into distant corners. For the most part, they're not afraid of the search, even when their discoveries are cobwebbed with confusion.

How many layers exist in a family or a life? It can be endless. We won't dwell too long in the past, because that can be paralyzing. Next week we'll dig a little deeper, then we'll wrap up our discoveries and new questions and carry them out of the cellars where we have been digging.

CHAPTER EIGHT

SECRETS TO KEEP
AND TELL

Secrets are things we give to others to keep for us.
—Elbert Hubbard

A friend called me recently and wanted to talk. Although her father had been dead for twenty years, she'd just learned some startling news about him. I had never known her father, but she had often spoken of him, not always kindly. He was basically a good man, she had told me, creative but volatile. She'd always had mixed feelings about their relationship. Now, she told me provocatively, she had learned something that put things in a different perspective.

We arranged to meet for dinner the following evening at a local restaurant, and when we were seated across from each other, had ordered our food, and were caught up on the latest news in each other's lives, she pulled out a sheaf of papers. "You're the only one I could tell about this," she said. "I'm not sure if I should talk to my mother or brothers." She smiled wryly. "I'm a big believer in the let-sleeping-dogs-lie philosophy of life. But this is really big, so I want you to tell me what you think."

My curiosity was piqued. "Of course."

"These papers," she said, "are my father's military records. I wrote for them a few months ago, and now that I've read them, I'm surprised they sent such detailed papers. He was in the army in World War Two, stationed in Italy, and we always knew that, but it was kind of vague what happened to him there. He never told us any war stories or showed pictures or anything. I always figured he had a 'normal' war experience—whatever that means. Well, according to these papers, two weeks after he arrived in Italy, he and his sergeant were driving a jeep and they hit a mine. The sergeant was killed and my father was only slightly injured. But it took three days for them to be found, and during that time my father flipped out—he was only eighteen years old. When they found him, he was sitting by the side of the road, cradling the dead sergeant in his arms. Apparently, he'd been like that for the entire three days."

"How horrible."

"Really! Imagine going through something like that when you're only eighteen. Anyway, the Army brought my dad back to the States and put him in a mental hospital, and he was there for the rest of the war. The hospital papers describe his condition as pretty serious—mentally, that is. Unfortunately, they didn't know about post-traumatic stress disorder then. The papers also say that he was engaged to be married before the war, but the woman left him after he'd been in the hospital for a year. She couldn't handle it. Unfortunately, they don't give her name." She paused a moment. "There's more. They also say my father's family had a history of insanity—both his grandmother and his sister were institutionalized at various times. They don't say which sister—I knew all three of my aunts fairly well, but there was never a mention of this. There was never a mention of any of it."

"You think your mother doesn't know?" I ask.

"I'm sure she doesn't. I've tried to feel her out subtly, and I can tell by her reaction that she has no idea. My mother never had a talent for pretense. She's too much of a blabbermouth. She definitely would have let it slip if she'd known. So I'm left sitting on top of a powder keg, not knowing what to do with this information."

"You're wondering whether to tell your mother and brothers?"

"Right. It could be a really bad idea, but maybe it would be helpful to my brothers. It certainly explains some things."

"How so?"

"When I read these papers, at first, I was just shocked. They seemed to be describing someone else. It was such a different picture of Dad than the one I had. You know, you go along with a certain family story all your life. You believe it and never question it. But the more I think about it, the more I realize that a lot of things about Dad never made sense. For instance, he'd often have violent bursts of temper that seemed to come from nowhere. He never hit us, but he was angry a lot. I basically stayed out of his way, but my brothers used to get into these rip-roaring fights with him. Now I think maybe it's all related to his keeping this big secret. I even think—this might be silly— that he got cancer from it."

"From keeping the secret?"

"Sure. The pressure must have been enormous. Nobody knew about this, not even my mother."

"His family must have known."

"I guess. But his parents were dead by the time he mar-

ried my mother, and his sisters weren't that close to us."
She shook her head helplessly, the disbelief shining in her
eyes. "My father managed to keep his distance from us,
but I never would have dreamed there was all this unknown
stuff going on."

"So, are you angry?" I asked her.

She looked surprised. "Angry? I don't know. Maybe a
little. More frustrated, really. I mean, it makes me wonder,
what else don't I know? And if my mother doesn't know—
which I'm sure of—what does it say about my parents'
relationship? There are so many unanswered questions."
She threw up her hands and nearly wailed, "Who keeps
such big secrets?"

The truth is, many people do, and the generational ethic
of post–World War II adults was especially strong to with-
hold bad news, to cover up family information that seemed
embarrassing, and to shield their loved ones—especially
children—from the harsh realities of life. It is not uncommon for people to admit to me that they knew little about
the details of their family history. They speak of parents
hedging about distant aunts, vaguely remembered scan-
dals, and family feuds. Even when grown-up children
press for more information, their pleas for the truth often
go unheeded. The subject is swiftly changed when the
uncomfortable question comes up.

Everyone has secrets, and sometimes it's appropriate to
keep them, since everyone deserves a piece of personal
privacy. The problem with keeping major secrets in a family is that the secret often lays a false foundation upon
which everything else is built.

I think of the woman who was told her parents were
divorced when she was young. All of her life, her mother
insisted she have nothing to do with her father, out of

loyalty to her mother. Even after she became an adult, her mother made a point of urging her not to have contact with him. Then, one day, she received word that her father was in the hospital dying. Should she go to him? She was deeply torn. It would be an act of disloyalty to her mother, and yet, how could she miss the opportunity? She finally decided to go. When she walked into her father's hospital room, her mother was sitting there holding his hand and telling her father she loved him. That was shocking enough, but later she found out they'd never been divorced.

She turned on her mother in a rage. "Disloyalty?" she shrieked. "You talk to me about disloyalty, and you never stopped loving him?" She later said, "In one moment, everything I had believed all my life had a different face."

Many of the big secrets people keep are in the interest of maintaining the appearance of having a spotless record in life, or of avoiding intimacy. A man once told me he thought it was perfectly correct for him to keep the amount of his salary a secret from his wife. More than likely, his secrecy about money was only one of the many imbalances in the relationship.

Over the years, I've talked with hundreds of adults who long to know more about their parents. But the question of what's known and what's a secret is more complicated than it seems at first glance. Sometimes the truth is so painful that people refuse to know it.

I think of the man who made a startling discovery after his beloved mother died. He was going through her trunk and he came upon an old photograph of his mother wearing a wedding gown, embracing a man he had never seen before. My patient was a man who had been deeply devoted to his mother and claimed to know everything about her. When he told me about his discovery, I was very interested. "It sounds like your mother was married before. Did you try to find out the truth by asking other relatives?"

"No," he replied evenly. "I tore up the picture."

Because he didn't want to accept the truth that was right before his eyes—indeed, he was unable to accept it—he simply negated it. No picture; no previous marriage.

In my work, I've encountered quite a few people who had shocking revelations after the death of a parent. Former marriages, causes of death, affairs, illnesses, children born out of wedlock, and other secrets haunt the survivors, who begin to question whether they knew their parent at all.

A woman who also discovered her mother was married before did not try to deny it by destroying the evidence. But she was quite distraught. "My mother and I were best friends. How could she keep it from me that she was married to someone else for five years before she even met my father?" she cried after finding the divorce papers among her mother's things.

Not all secrets revealed from beyond the grave are negative. A woman in one of my groups was astonished to find a whole box of awards and commendations her mother had earned by doing volunteer work. "My mother was always on the go, but I never paid any attention to what she was doing," she told me, marveling at the extent of her mother's contribution to the community. "Now I find out she was practically Mother Teresa!"

Another woman was shocked when so many people showed up at her father's funeral. "He always said he didn't have very many friends, and he was lonely. But there were all these people who said they were his friends."

In other cases, a revelation can explain previously con-fusing behavior and help bring an estranged adult child to a point of peace. A disc jockey in a major city once de-scribed such a serendipitous experience. He had cut himself off from his parents most of his adult life, moving to another city and having very little to do with them. In particular, he resented his mother, whom he judged to be a very negative, unpleasant woman. When she died, he didn't know how to feel. But soon after her death, he received a package in the mail from an old friend of his mother's. The cover letter explained that these were letters his mother had written to the friend many years ago, and she thought he might like to have them. When he began to read them, he suddenly saw his mother in a new way. She confided to her friend how hard it was to live with an alcoholic (he never knew that about his father!) and how much the family struggled to get by (he never knew that, either). Now he had a different perspective on his mother's unhappiness. Much was explained.

Sometimes, revelations are made in my group that have an unexpected impact. I remember the time a woman came to the group session one evening and announced that she'd just had the shock of her life. "I found out my father was married before," she told us. "I can't believe this—it's just too amazing. I have a half brother living in Europe. I'm fifty years old, and I never knew I had a brother." She was close to tears. "How could he decide not to tell me this? He thought it was none of my business that I had a brother? Now I wonder, what else don't I know?"

There was a gasp across the room and we all turned to look at another woman whose face was turning white. "I can't believe this," she cried. "My husband was married before and he also had a child by his first wife. They're not in touch at all. We've talked about it and decided our son doesn't need to know."

The two women stared at each other and there was great tension in the room. Finally, the second woman said, "Listening to you, I'm telescoping ahead to a time in the future when our son makes the same discovery. Now I understand that we have to tell him he has a half sister. This is not something we have a right to keep from him." (A footnote to this story: I encountered this woman a year later and she admitted with some embarrassment that they still hadn't told the child.)

In the same way that children often don't know the deep secrets that might give them clues about who their parents really were, the parents may never have known important things about their adult children. Of course, we all know children don't tell their parents all the details of their lives— and it's a good thing, too, because most parents would have heart failure if they knew about every adventure. Again, it's important to distinguish between privacy and secrecy. In some ways, privacy is something you can choose. It's no one else's business. Secrets are more likely the things you want to hide because of the consequences of telling. It feels like a choice. Every person has a private self that no one else can penetrate. No parent knows all there is to know about a child—even the ones who brag that they can read their child's mind.

But when I talk to adult children who have lost a parent, I am often saddened by the suffering of those who regret having withheld significant confidences from their parents. They often say, "My mother [or father] never knew the real me, and now I won't have a chance to show her [or him]."

There are many reasons adult children don't tell their parents important things. Perhaps they don't want to disappoint them or worry them or get into arguments they know will be futile. By the same token, some parents choose to turn the other way and not "know" what they know. They deliberately refrain from asking questions so they won't hear the answers.

The more secrets there are, the more closed the family becomes, and the deeper the regrets. People have often told me they had secrets they planned to tell someday, and were very sad when their parents died before they had a chance.

"My father never knew I got a dishonorable discharge from the navy," a middle-aged Vietnam veteran told me. "I was caught doing drugs. I was young and screwed up, but Dad was a navy man and I thought if he knew at the time, he would have killed me. Later, I thought about telling him on several occasions, but the right time never seemed to come up."

"My parents never knew I had an illegal abortion when I was a teenager," a woman revealed. "The whole incident is still fresh in my mind. I was so terrified. I cried the whole time and really wanted my mother there with me. Years later, I almost told her. We were discussing the abortion issue and she was strongly prochoice. But it was too late to tell the truth, because I believed she would have been hurt that I didn't come to her then. So I let the moment pass."

"My mother thought I was perfect," another woman told me. "I wonder what she would have said if she'd known I used to steal small amounts of money out of her purse and use the money to buy cigarettes. Now it seems like a small deceit—the kind of thing kids do. But if she'd known, she might have seen me more realistically. I always walked on eggshells so I'd be the perfect daughter she thought I was. Deep down, I wished she'd find out so I would know if she'd love me anyway, even if I wasn't perfect."

Many children are burdened with the weight of secrets adults have told them not to reveal. One man recalled seeing his father shoplift when he was a young boy. He adored his father and could hardly believe his own eyes. His father swore him to secrecy, and it weighed on his mind for thirty years. Finally, after his father was long dead, he blurted out the secret to his mother, only to discover that she had known all along about her husband's shoplifting problem.

In a child's view, something may seem like a secret when it really isn't. Then again, sometimes it feels safer to believe something is secret. A man once said, "I never told my mother that my father beat me with a belt when I was about four years old."

I was surprised. "Don't you think your mother knew?"

"No," he insisted. "Dad always did it when she was out."

"Didn't she see the marks on your back when she bathed you?"

He shook his head. "No, she never did."

Even faced with an irrefutable idea—how could she not see?—he couldn't allow himself to let it be true.

Sometimes, the secrets are very serious. A woman came to me emotionally distraught, many years after her parents had died. "They loved me so much," she said. "They would have done anything to protect me. But I never told them my uncle raped me when I was eleven. At the time, I was confused, and I think I thought they wouldn't believe me. It ruined my life for many years and they never knew. I know now they would have been on my side. They would have made sure I got help. But I never gave them the chance."

One man revealed that he had never told his parents he was homosexual. "We were the perfect Ozzie and Harriet Midwest family," he said ruefully. "I was your average kid, except that from the time I was fourteen I knew I was gay. It terrified me and thrilled me—it was such a huge secret. I never even considered telling my parents. Instead, I moved to New York, where I could live my own life. When we'd talk, I'd tell them everything that was going on, except the main thing. It always hurt me that I was living a lie. At times, I thought it unfair to them; it was certainly unfair to me. But I didn't have the courage to let them really know me."

As evidence that telling big secrets does not always have predictable results, another gay man recalled finally telling his parents the truth. "My dad was a minister and my mom was a schoolteacher. I expected the worst. But my dad had cancer and he wasn't going to be around much longer. I decided I had to tell them. I chose my moment very carefully and finally made the announcement, shaking like a leaf the entire time. My mom said, 'Oh, honey, we've always known—but we're glad you told us.' "

He cried when he recalled that moment, and now that his parents are no longer alive, he said he felt more peaceful knowing he had let them into his life and they had accepted him.

Sometimes people aren't even aware of how the secrets they keep from their parents make a difference in their relationships. I remember having a woman in therapy who described in glowing detail how close she and her father were. Her mother had died many years earlier, and the two of them had become a team. She boasted that she knew everything about him and he knew everything about her—except for one thing. She never told him that she had undergone two major cancer operations. I was startled by the admission, and I asked how she had kept such major events secret from a man to whom she was so close. She proudly described a complex scheme of duplicity and deceit. "It took work, but I managed," she said.

"But why?" I asked.

Her explanation was that she didn't want to worry him. "He would have been terrified." I thought how sad it was that people think they have to protect their loved ones from the truth, when so often the truth can be liberating. She denied her father the opportunity to offer comfort, and she denied herself the opportunity to be comforted. And in the process, she never considered what the consequences might be for him had he found out: What if he'd learned she was in the hospital? What if she had died?

In the group, we talk about secrets. I take the opportunity to talk about open and closed family systems. "Sometimes people protect themselves by not asking questions because they get the message the answers might be too traumatic," I say. "If you have questions you've never asked in your family, what are the consequences of asking? And what are the consequences of knowing the answers? If you had the opportunity to ask your deceased parent one question, what would it be, and what would it allow you to know about your parent, yourself, and your family?" I ask. There is silence while they mull this over. I've had groups where every person draws a blank; people shrug and say, "No questions." "Nope, I know everything." "There's nothing in particular I can think of." This group, I'm pleased to see, is a bit more forthcoming.

"I would ask my father to tell me about his concentration camp experiences," says Patricia thoughtfully. "Just recently, I attended a conference for children of survivors of the Holocaust, and I can't tell you the regret I felt at not having my father's personal memories—even though it would have been painful for him to talk about and painful for me to hear. Now those experiences are lost to me, my son, and future generations forever."

"Can you ask your mother to fill in some of the blanks?" I ask.

"Since the conference, I've been trying, but I have to approach it carefully, like a detective. She's uncomfortable talking about the past, and it mystifies her that I suddenly have so many questions. It's ironic: She wants to forget the past and I want to remember it. Of course, it's possible, likely even, that Papa never told her very many details about his experience. He was a very circumspect man, and it would have been his way to try and shield her from hearing such gruesome stories. But it's very important to me. This is history—my own and the world's."

"I can relate to the idea of wanting information about your family history," Richard says. "Since my father died, I've been hungry for details about the family. My mother isn't much help, but fortunately, my father's older sister has taken it upon herself to be the family historian. I just found out from her that my father's grandfather landed at Ellis Island and is listed in the register there. And my mother's great-uncle fought in the Civil War. Her side of the family has been here for over a hundred and fifty years. She didn't even know it until I told her!" He grins proudly.

"I tell you, it's an exhilarating experience which has brought history alive for me. You never think of your family as being part of history." He turns to address Patricia. "Your father had a personal experience, but he was also part of a great historical moment that changed the future of a whole race of people."

"I know. And to think I let him die without telling me about it." She sighs, annoyed with herself for missing the opportunity.

"I don't know if there are any big secrets in my family," Richard says. "But I did learn something recently that changed my perspective a little. I always tended to think of my parents as just parents, not real people—if you get the difference. They acted the way I figured parents acted, and I didn't question it. When I was growing up, they were just there. The only thing different about my family from those of my friends was that my dad worked late a lot. Otherwise, it was normal. I never wondered what they were feeling or what they talked about in private. I never thought about what their lives were like before they got married and started having kids. I probably would have believed it if someone told me my mom came to earth fully hatched as a mom. Anyway, a couple weeks ago, she happened to mention she was once engaged to another man before she met Dad. It blew my mind. You'd have to know my mother! I started thinking, wow, my parents were young, they met, they fell in love. Just like people." The awe in Richard's voice is comical. We all laugh and he joins in. "It's like the saying that all kids know their parents had sex at least once, but they still sort of hope the stork brought them," he says.

"You're describing something universal," I tell Richard.

"There's a reason. Children need to see their parents as omnipotent, not human. It makes them feel safe. It's hard to make the adult transition to suddenly seeing parents as flesh-and-blood creatures."

I look around the circle. "Anyone else have a question they'd ask a parent?"

"My mother's father died before I was born," Amanda says, "and no one ever talked about what caused his death. I always assumed cancer or a heart attack or something. It was all kept very hush-hush, and since I never knew him, I didn't have much curiosity about it. Well, not long ago, my father was visiting for the weekend, and we were talking about the recession, and suddenly he drops this bombshell that my mother's father committed suicide in the thirties following the stock-market crash. He jumped out of a window. Can you believe it? Apparently, this was a shameful family secret that nobody ever talked about. I'd sure love to have a chance to ask my mother about that."

"If my father was alive today, I'd ask him why he threw hot coffee all over me when I was seven years old," Eileen says solemnly. "What was he thinking? Why was he doing it? I'd like to know."

"Do you think there's an answer to that question?" I ask. "Or an explanation? There's no acceptable explanation for pouring hot coffee on a child. Do you think you did something to cause it?"

"Of course not. He was drunk." She looks defeated. "I guess I want answers to questions that have no answers."

"So do I," Jane says loudly. "I want to ask my mother if she committed suicide, or if it was an accident. Sometimes I think I'll die if I don't know the truth." Her eyes are shining with tears and fury. "I've been over this in my mind a million times, and I keep reaching the same conclusion: I can't prove it, but my gut tells me she did."

The group is momentarily frozen in silence, not sure how to handle this new information. "How do you think it would help you to know for sure?" I ask.

"Then I could deal with it. I could say, OK, my mother was a suicide. It's worse not to know. When people ask how she died, I tell them it was an accident, but my mind always says, 'Maybe suicide.' This was a woman who was supposedly my best friend in the world, and maybe she killed herself in my apartment. It's too much."

"You have said your mother was a troubled woman. . . ."

"Right. And she was also very ill. I don't think she would have lived very long anyway. But suicide . . . I don't know, it's such an ugly, lonely thing."

I tell her, "When a parent or anyone close to you commits suicide, that's perhaps one of the most difficult death to overcome. It's natural to let your mind run on with 'what ifs,' and to feel guilty about all the things you might have done. But your mother made a choice. Can you see that choice as being separate from and without consideration for you?"

Jane is sobbing. "In our church, it's a mortal sin to commit suicide. I can't bear the thought that my mother is burning in hell forever."

"Maybe you should talk to your priest about it," I suggest.

Richard reaches over and takes Jane's hand. "I'm Catholic, too," he says warmly. "I believe in God's mercy."

The room is very still. Barry says quietly, "I have a big secret." Everyone turns to look at him with interest. "I'm gay," he says. "I don't care if anyone in this room knows. The point is, I never told my dad or anyone else in my family. I wish I'd told my dad. I really do."

"You could tell the rest of your family," Richard suggests. "That might make you feel better."

"I plan to," Barry says. "But I'll never have a chance to tell Dad; that's the main thing."

"What do you think would have been different had he known?" I ask.

That stumps him. "I don't know, but it feels like I've been living a lie."

"Maybe you could express it in a letter to him," I suggest. "Next week, during our final session, we'll explore how you ritualize your parent's death. One idea is to write a letter to that person. You can say good-bye, tell a secret, or anything else that comes to mind. Remember, letting go of your dead parent is not the same as forgetting."

"I feel like we need about ten or twenty more sessions," Arlene grumbles.

"That's what people usually say." I smile at her. "Don't worry. This isn't the end. Far from it. You might say it's only the beginning."

———————————— ▬▬▬ ————————————

CHAPTER NINE

SAYING GOOD-BYE

Death takes away. That's all there is to
it. But grief gives back. By experiencing
it, we are not simply eroded by pain. Rather,
we become larger human beings, more compassionate.
more aware, more able to help others,
more able to help ourselves.
         —Candy Lightner

Our final meeting together has the bittersweet feeling of a farewell party. We'll be saying good-bye to one another, and also to the whole cast of supporting characters, including the parents who have died and other family members. Several people have brought photographs of their parents, and we pass them around the circle, remarking on them as if we are seeing old friends—which, in a sense, we are. Our time together has been brief, but the bonding has been intense. I suspect the people in this room will never forget one another; the stories they shared will linger in people's memories and continue to offer insight and comfort long after we have disbanded.

"So, this is our final week," I say as I look around the group and catch each person's eye. I hope my voice communicates something of the genuine fondness I feel for them. "Our task tonight is to talk about letting go. You may have decided to write a letter to your parent, or have thought of some other ritual. Some of you may think you're not ready yet. If that's the case, it's helpful to ask, 'What's the next step I can take?' Who would like to begin?"

"I will," Patricia volunteers. "Yesterday, I sent my son to a friend's house so I could be alone. I felt very melancholy. Writing this letter . . . it had been on my mind all week. I still didn't know what I was going to say. I finally decided to see what would happen if I just sat down and started writing. I cleared the desk of all my other papers and got out my best stationary. My desk is positioned so it looks out the window to our backyard. The trees are all bare of leaves now, but there are still big piles on the ground. Papa always made an event of raking the leaves. I just let them go this year. I wrote this letter to him." She blushes. "Frankly, I didn't know I had all of these thoughts until I went to put them on paper." She reads:

> Dear Papa,
> You have been in my thoughts every day since you died. Your death was unexpected, so I never got a chance to give you a hug and kiss and say good-bye. To tell you the truth, maybe I wouldn't have even if there had been a chance. Hugs and kisses were never very big in our family. But yesterday I gave Mama a big hug and told her I loved her. I didn't want to miss the chance. You might have laughed a little if you had seen this sight. She was shocked! She asked me if there was something wrong with me, and I told her no, I just wanted her to know how I felt. She blushed bright red, but I think she was pleased.
> Displays of affection always came hard for us, didn't they? But I never for one minute doubted the size of our love for each other. You and Mama had many experiences in your life that I could not even begin to grasp.

I've always believed these experiences placed a curtain around your emotions. I want you to know I respect that, and I've never wanted you to be any different. (And maybe if I did, just a little, it was when I was young and didn't know all the things I know now.)

There are many things I wish I knew about your life, but I understand you had your reasons for keeping them private. Maybe you wanted to spare us any of the hurt you suffered. But now, in memory of you, I'm taking it upon myself to learn as much as I can about the past. It's my way of remembering you.

You have given me so much, it would be impossible to list everything. Just know that I love you and will miss you forever. So will Joel. I'm grateful he had the opportunity to have a grandfather like you. Earlier today, I finally found and read the letter you wrote to him right before you died. You know, he didn't receive it in the mail until you were gone, and I've never been able to bring myself to read it until now. Well, I read it, and there was your voice. Talking about how pretty the beach was, the colorful shells you collected, the funny water bicycles you saw people riding. It was an ordinary letter from an ordinary day. I think about you and I realize you had many such ordinary days, just as we all do. But you have also had some quite extraordinary days. Your ability to rise above your past and appreciate the joys of life even after you experienced such a great tragedy has taught me a lesson I will always try to remember, and make sure Joel remembers, too.

Good-bye, Papa. I love you. Patricia.

Tears stream down Patricia's cheeks as she finishes reading. We are all moved. Silently, I pass the box of tissues around the circle. Patricia says, "I'm crying, but it's not because I'm sad, at least not in the same way. This is hard to explain, but I feel released. Saying good-bye to Papa was so final, but writing the letter made me feel good.

Some of the things I said—I could never have said them to him when he was alive. But I feel as if he knows them now because I've written this letter. Does that make any sense?"

Several people around the circle are nodding. She adds, "I put my promise down on paper to start exploring our history. It made it concrete."

Jane is sitting with her head in her hands. "Jane?" I ask.

She looks up; her face is red and blotchy with tears and exhaustion. "Sorry," she sniffs. "I was just thinking."

"About . . . ?"

"I've been going through a lot. It's been like walking into a burning building. The pain of thinking about my parents has been excruciating. But so much of the pain was because of what was left unsaid between us. After last week, talking about my mom's suicide—or the possibility of it—I couldn't stop crying for two days. I wasn't sure if I could stand to know the truth. Now I know why people keep secrets! I started planning my letter and how I'd ask her about it. But I was afraid she'd answer me, and I wouldn't be able to stand the answer."

"What would she say that you wouldn't be able to stand?" I ask softly.

She stops to blow her nose. "Oh, gee . . . I guess she'd say she couldn't bear to go on living. She was too unhappy. Even I couldn't make her happy. Even knowing how much I would suffer . . . it wouldn't be enough."

I tread gently. Suicide is a snakepit for the griever. In addition to losing the one you love, there are so many other feelings: guilt that you couldn't save the person; hurt that your love wasn't enough to make the person want to live; anger that the person could choose to leave you like this. "Jane, do you feel you could have saved her?"

She shakes her head no, then doesn't look so sure. "I don't know. Rationally, I know I couldn't have. I've dealt with suicides at the hospital. I always tell the survivors not to blame themselves. But this isn't rational. My mind says it wasn't my fault, but my heart says, I'm not so sure."

"What about your mother? Do you wonder how she could have done this to you? Are you angry?"

"I don't know that, either. Lately, as I've reached a fuller understanding of my mother and come to realize she was so unhappy, I see more. Maybe she couldn't take it—being so sick and weak and unhappy."

"Did you talk to your priest?" Richard asks her.

Jane nods. "He was wonderful! He doesn't agree with the hellfire and brimstone theory of religion, and he put some of my fears to rest. He asked me to come and talk with him again, and I think I will. But I wish there were more weeks in this group."

"You've opened the door and started to look inside, but it can be a beginning," I tell her.

She sighs, having reached the same conclusion herself.

"Does anyone else have a letter or a thought to share?" I ask.

"This was quite an experience," Barry says. "I decided, well, better late than never—I'd tell my dad I was gay. Putting it in a letter to him was strange. I almost felt he was looking over my shoulder." Barry begins the letter:

Dear Dad,
  On the day you died, I never had a chance to say good-bye. It was because I was afraid to stay and watch you die. So I ran home and hid. Boy, I felt so bad about that, even though everyone else was great. Anyway, I miss you a lot. This week, I was replaying the scene from your last day, only this time I'm in the room with

you. I'm sitting by your bed, and I lean over and kiss you and tell you I love you, and you squeeze my hand. That's the way I wish it could have been.

I have a lot of wishes that won't come true now because you're gone. A lot of missed opportunities and regrets. You always told me to live life fully because it could be snatched away at any time. I know you believed that and you lived that way. I wasn't always so courageous. I think you might have suspected I was gay, but you never said anything, and neither did I. Being gay in this day and age is a constant encounter with mortality, and this is something I would have liked to talk to you about. I've seen friends die of AIDS, and sometimes I'm afraid for myself. I never gave you a chance to accept me, but I like to think you would have.

I realize now that I've always been gay, but I didn't really know it or admit it to myself until two years ago. By then, you were already quite sick. That's my excuse for not telling you. I didn't want to be the cause of any unhappiness in your life or any worry. But now, I think I was wrong to keep this secret, because it interferred with our being close, and our love for each other is something I've always cherished and been proud of.

Am I happy? (I know you'd ask.) The answer is yes and no. I've been very sad since you died, but I've been staying with a man who is very supportive, and he's helping me to get through it. I'm starting to learn to be more open, and that's a good thing. When I see how brief your life was, I want to make every moment count.

I love you. You're in my heart. Good-bye for now.

Your son, Barry.

Barry folds the letter solemnly. "I'm sorry I never told him," he says. "I think he would have been OK about it. But now I've decided no more lies. I'm going to show this letter to my mother and sisters and start being honest."

"How do you think they'll react?" I ask.

"OK, actually. They're good people. Maybe they already suspect—they're not stupid. Right now, they just want me to be happy, and everyone has been quite concerned about my reaction to Dad's death. They'll be relieved to see I'm getting on with my life. That's the important thing."

"Good luck," I say. "It sounds like you feel good about the decision. Anyone else?"

"Last week, my husband and I were talking about our plans to have a child someday," Eileen says suddenly. I turn to look at her, and she seems more subdued tonight—tired, not fiesty. "It's a conversation we regularly have, and, you know . . . I think I've said here, how great my concern has been about bringing a child into this crazy family of mine. But Frederick really wants a child. Our conversation brought all my feelings back. I thought about writing a letter to my mother, or to my father, but what's the point? I've already said everything a million times and no one listened before."

I tell her, "When you write a letter to a parent who has died, you're talking to yourself as much as you are to that person. Maybe you have things you want to tell yourself."

She shrugs. "Like what?"

"Well, you want to fix everything in your family; you feel responsible for fixing it. Maybe you need to tell yourself to let it go, let your brother and sister live as they've chosen, let the past be past. . . . "

"I'll think about it," she says. "That's what I'd like to do. I feel as if I'm carrying around a hundred-pound weight. But it's not so easy, you know?"

"I know." I pause for a moment to let the emotion sit. Then I ask, "Anyone else?"

Richard's face looks eased of some of the strain and sheer

tiredness he's been showing all along. "I did a crazy thing, on a whim," he says almost brightly. "I went home last week, and I was thinking about this letter and about everything else that was going on, and right out of the blue, while we were sitting around the dinner table, I just started telling my wife and mother about it." He grins. "My mother nearly dropped her soup spoon! I've been tiptoeing around her—we all have—and not daring to mention a word about my father for fear it would upset her too much. But I was feeling daring that night. I talked about the group and some of the things we discussed, and about this letter I wanted to write to Dad. At first, she just didn't get it. She said, 'How can you write him a letter? He's dead.' My wife and I started laughing—you had to be there; the look on my mother's face was so hilarious— and that broke the ice. I got up from my seat and went over and gave her a big smack on the cheek. She was embarrassed. She didn't have the slightest idea what all of this was about."

"Did you talk more about the letter after that?"

"No. And I never wrote it—I will. I've come to the conclusion that I can't grieve for Dad until I've dealt with my mother."

"It's part of the same puzzle," I say. "Remember our conversation about family systems?"

"Let me put it this way: My mother is the more immediate issue."

"If your father were sitting here, what would you say to him about your mother?"

"Whew!" He looks genuinely surprised. "There's a question! Um . . . 'Thanks a lot for leaving me with this mess'? No, really, I'd tell him . . . I don't know. I have to think about it."

"You don't have to do it now." I let him off the hook. "The reason it's useful is that it can help you say things out loud to yourself that you may have been unable to give voice to before."

"I can see that." Richard, always eager to consider a new idea, is nodding his head enthusiastically. "I promise to try it. Oh, by the way. We just found out my brother is coming from London for the holidays. It should be interesting. We haven't really talked since the funeral. I think it's time we had a heart-to-heart about what we're going to do with Mom. I've decided it's time to be less in charge. Perhaps I haven't left room for him." He smiles mischievously. "I have in mind a little international trip for her very soon."

"That sounds like a great idea." I smile at him. He's doing fine. "Anyone else?"

Marian says shyly, "I'm not ready to write a letter. I'm not good at letters anyway. What would I say? I still feel so bad and I don't want Mom to hear it."

"How do you think she would react if she knew how bad you were feeling?"

"She never liked sadness around the house."

This is an interesting route. I decide to explore it a little.

"There was sadness when your parents got a divorce, wasn't there?"

She nods. "Uh-huh. But Mom didn't want Jack and me to feel bad about it. She said it was between her and Dad and wasn't because of us."

"Maybe it wasn't because of you. But it affected you."

"Well, of course it did. I hated it."

"Did you ever tell your mother or your father how you felt?"

"Sort of. But they had their own problems. Just before

she died, Mom had started going out socially. I was old enough where we could really start talking. But that's over."

She sits with her mouth half open like she wants to say more. "What else?" I ask.

"It's about Mrs. Gibson—Marge," she says shyly. "Jack and I were talking last week. He said, 'If Marge hadn't been the one who did it'—you know, hit my mom—'she would have been around to help now. It's like a double loss.' It's true. It's all confused, you know. We loved Marge." She looks to me for help.

"Part of your healing might be talking to your neighbor," I suggest. "When you think you're ready."

"Uh-huh." She wiggles her leg frantically. "OK ... maybe soon."

My heart goes out to her. Her wound is still very fresh. "Does anyone else want to share?"

"I'm still working on my letter," says Irene apologetically. "I started to do it, and it was harder than I thought it would be. Then I realized I also had things to say to my mother, and she's been dead for twenty years. For one thing, I'd ask her why she let herself go? How could she get so fat. I don't understand how anyone could have so little self-respect."

I've noticed how trim and fit Irene is. "What do you think she would say if you asked her?"

"I don't know," she answers honestly. "It's beyond my power to imagine why anyone would do that. I guess she had no self-control. She couldn't help herself. My father used to try. If she was eating something bad for her, he'd make a point of it. But she wouldn't listen."

"Maybe he was the last person she could listen to," I

suggest. "People overeat for a lot of reasons. It's not necessarily a matter of self-control. Maybe this is a line of exploration you can pursue."

She squeezes her eyes shut. "It's not very pleasant, but I suppose you're right."

"It might tell you why you feel you need to be so controlled and responsible," I say. "And then, perhaps, it will give you an idea about what to do next."

"I had the exact same experience," Helen says. "I mean, of thinking about my mother. She's been dead twenty-four years, but she's on my mind almost more than my father. What do you think it means?"

"The important thing is, what do *you* think it means?" I reply.

"I know, I know. I have a lot of work to do. But you'll be glad to know my husband thinks I've been more chipper lately. He said the other night, 'This is the old Helen.' I figured it out that I was still grieving because I wanted to grieve. Now I don't want to anymore."

"Well," I tell her, "it is true that we always have choices, even when it seems things are beyond our control. But sometimes what helps to break us loose is the process of examination, which has been our task here. Some of the stuff you've put in the closet is coming out now. Even when it's painful, sometimes there's a lightening of the load."

I see that Arlene looks lost in thought as she sits, twisting her engagement ring around her finger. "Arlene?" I ask.

"I pass," she says in a whispery, tired voice. "I wouldn't even know where to begin. Please, don't make me."

"You want to still be sad?"

"It's not a matter of wanting to. It's what is. I may never stop being sad. I don't think you appreciate what kind of relationship we had." She launches into the familiar oratory about her sainted father, as the others in the group begin to look impatient. I decide to let it go. This is a job for long-term therapy, not a support group. I have to balance Arlene's need with the needs of the others. In a sense, she never really joined this group. To fully be a part of the group experience, one has to be open to sharing and to listening, and Arlene has done neither. I motion to Matt.

"I couldn't write anything," says Matt staring at his hands in despair. "The idea of saying good-bye . . . it was too impossible. I'm starting to feel like the 'F' student in this class."

"That's OK." I gaze at his troubled face intently. "The letter is just a tool. Maybe you need to do something else first. Take it one step at a time. It's only been a few months. Who else? Mary Ann?"

She shakes her head. "I don't know what to say."

"OK, how about this. Can you think of what would be the next step for you?"

She considers my question and seems to draw a blank.

"How about Thanksgiving? The whole family will be there. It's going to be quite an event, and probably a strain, without your mother. Can you try to be an observer of your family dynamics? Make that your task. See what you can learn. It may seem to be unrelated to your feelings about your mother's death, but you'll probably learn something from watching."

She agrees to do that, and jots a note in the pad she's holding in her lap.

I glance at my watch. "We don't have very much time left, and it seems as though there is still so much to say," I note with regret. "But I want to talk a little bit about the future and start you on the journey you still have to travel.

"Some of you might be surprised that we're here in our final session and there are still so many questions remaining. I told you in the beginning this would happen, but each person comes into a group like this with his or her own expectations. You didn't really know then what you hoped to gain from the group; maybe you're not sure now how you go about taking the next step. The immediate future may still be a blurry uncertainty. So what I'd like each of you to do, as an assignment to take with you, is to find a quiet time to sit and consider this question: As you imagine yourself five years from now, what do you see? Take your time and look around. What do you look like? Where are you living? Who's with you? What are you doing? See if you can envision yourself as the person who is no longer grieving every day for your lost parent or parents. Who is that person?

"In some respects, when a parent dies, you are forced to create a fresh identity for yourself, because a vital link has been severed. If you take this imaginary leap into the distant future, you might be able to see yourself more clearly."

"Five years from now—that's so hard to imagine!" Amanda exclaims.

"It probably seems that way, until you start doing it," I agree. "Part of what you are doing is setting goals. You're telling yourself how you'd like to be. Amanda, you have said several times in the group that you would like to be married. Maybe your picture of yourself five years from now will be that of a married woman." I smile at her and she smiles back. "And maybe not. It's up to you. When you visualize your life in five years, you are really making a decision. That decision is how you will ultimately respond to this great loss you have experienced. Then you can go back and ask what changes you need to make to reach that point."

"I wish my mother could do this exercise," Patricia says wistfully.

"Well, anyone can do it. But it's not something you jump right into. If I had asked you to do this the first time we met, before we had been through any of our other discussions, I imagine your response would have been quite different. Some of you may not be ready to do it yet—" I stop and look at Matt.

He sighs heavily. "I know I've been a pain in the ass here," he admits. "This has been very difficult for me, and maybe fighting the process has been my way of refusing to accept this." He smiles, a rare sight. "Like an incorrigible child, huh?"

"When we come to the end of a group, I always feel a great pressure to say something profound that will tie together in a neat bundle all we've been through," I tell them. "But whenever I try to think of what that meaningful remark might be, I realize once again what I've known all along: The profound insights in this room come from you, not from me. Life itself, in its confusing, often painful, occasionally inspirational moments, is what is profound. The road you're traveling, from life to death and back to life again, is the same road every human being travels. It's not something we keep in our consciousness all the time, but it's the great truth we've been facing here, and what you'll take away with you: the awareness that we are mortal and that life is a series of good-byes. And sometimes with those good-byes come new beginnings."

CHAPTER TEN

LESSONS IN HEALING

Man is born broken. He lives by
mending. The grace of God is glue.
—Eugene O'Neill

You are the child whose parent is gone forever, the "orphaned" son or daughter struggling to cope with your grief. You may recognize yourself in many of the stories that have been shared in this book. If so, I hope reading it has helped you feel less alone and powerless. It has been my experience that people are helped by hearing what others in similar situations have been through, and learning how they've managed to reintegrate their lives and move on.

Now, I'd like you to focus on your own situation. The exercises in this chapter are designed to help you on your journey to healing. Some are based on the exercises I do with my groups, and others on the work I do in my private practice. They have all been found useful by people at various stages of the grief process. I'm including them because they might be helpful to you.

But before you begin, let me stress that mourning is

different for each person. You might not be ready to do most or any of the exercises here. If any of them are too difficult or upsetting, please set them aside. If it seems too scary to do this work alone, find a partner—a spouse, friend, or sibling whom you trust or who has experienced a similar loss. If you're presently in therapy, you might want to show the exercises to your therapist before you begin on your own. Maybe he or she would be willing to work on them with you.

If your parent's death is recent, you're probably still feeling too involved in your mourning and may simply be unready to move to another point. I urge you to view these exercises simply as possible aids to your recovery— whether you do them now or put the book away and pick it up in a few months.

When you're ready to look at the exercises, take as much time as you need. You'll want to purchase a special note-book for the purpose of writing down your reflections and feelings.

Whether you're ready to do the exercises or not, I urge you to make time to grieve, especially if your parent's death was recent. This can help you alleviate some of the panic. It might be every day at first, then every few days. This is basically what we do in my groups and what I offer in my private practice—a time set aside for grieving. It's something the world is reluctant to allow you.

One woman who was grieving over the death of her mother once told me how hard she had tried to maintain control of her life, afraid that her sad feelings might spill out at odd moments. She was an extremely demure person, and it felt highly improper to impose her feelings on others. She decided on her own that the best thing to do was to set aside one hour every day when she could freely think about her mother, cry, be angry, or express any other feelings she wanted to. She made a pact with herself that this would be her time, and she pointedly postponed thinking about her mother except for the special period she had reserved.

Soon after making this agreement with herself, she was riding a bus and overheard two women talking about their mothers. She described the moment graphically. "It was really amazing," she told me later. "I felt a wave of heat pass over me that exploded off my face. I was completely riveted by their conversation, totally focused on every nuance and inflection as they blithely went on. Suddenly, I missed my mother so much I could feel the muscles in my face quivering, and my eyes filled with tears. I wanted to jump off the bus and run crying down the street. But then I remembered I'd made a deal with myself. Just knowing I could remember the moment and cry later during the hour that I had set aside for that purpose really helped me to calm down. I was able to stay on the bus and go to work."

This woman found her own method for dealing with the powerful feelings of grief. It may not work the same way for you. The point is, even if no one else is willing to do so, you can give yourself permission to feel what you are feeling. And it might help if you have a special time and place reserved to do that.

Exercise 1: ACKNOWLEDGE THE LOSS

Remember, grief takes energy. In the beginning, it is assumed you are not expected to meet all of your obligations. In fact, religions build this understanding into their rituals;

services treat mourners as fragile beings. Now, consider the ways in which you are allowing yourself the necessary time and space to mourn. What about your life reflects that a change has occurred?

What do you do now that gives you solace? For example:

> being with someone else
> listening to music
> talking to yourself
> reading a book
> changing your environment
> other examples?

What do you allow yourself not to do? For example:

> chores
> work
> charity
> comforting others
> talking with friends
> other examples?

Exercise 2: PRACTICE SAYING NO

People will want to fix your grief for you. They may be perfectly well-meaning, or they may be impatient with how long it's taking you to get over your loss. (For some people, anything more than two weeks is too long!) Remember, it isn't your job to make them feel better by acquiescing to their plans for your recovery. Your job is to take care of yourself.

Most people have trouble saying no, especially when it's

to friends who are trying to help. But if a friend urges you to come out for a party because she thinks it will cheer you up, or have guests over, or go to a movie, or talk when you don't feel like talking—learn to say no without worrying that you are hurting your friend's feelings.

As hard as it may be, you must sometimes also say no to people who are grieving for the same person you are—siblings or a surviving parent. It's also not your job to be the one who takes care of everybody else. For example, the woman who never expressed her own grief over the death of her father because she was so busy taking care of her mother—whom she described as a "basket case"—needed to know that her primary responsibility was to herself. If you have trouble with that idea because you've always been the "good soldier" in your family or the one who naturally looked out for everyone else's well-being, it might help to realize that you can't help another person find the way when you yourself are lost. But it may be unhelpful to support someone else instead of beginning your own work.

Exercise 3: ASK FOR HELP

You may discover that you are gravitating toward a certain person who really seems to help you. Maybe it's the friend who is willing to just listen instead of giving advice. Or the person who lifts your spirits in any one of a dozen ways. You may feel that sharing your burden with others makes you seem weak or needy. But it never ceases to amaze me how generous others can be in times of need. Try to identify what gives you comfort, then seek it.

It may be especially helpful to spend time with people who knew your parent—including a parent's longtime or childhood friends. If you can't do that, find a place where you can connect with others who share your experience in some way.

Exercise 4: ARTICULATE YOUR UNCENSORED FEELINGS

Some people find that writing in a journal is the best way to express their feelings. A journal is private, for your eyes only; no one has to read it but you. You can write about your sadness, fear, anger, relief, or ambivalence.

If writing down your feelings strikes you as being uncomfortable or too upsetting, another medium might work better. For example, I know a woman who started making collages after her mother died. She didn't know how to express her feelings directly, so she started going through newspapers and magazines and cutting out pictures, words, and phrases that expressed her thoughts. In the process of making collages, she discovered a creative, artistic side she never knew she possessed.

Exercise 5: USE MEMORIES TO HEAL

When you're ready—and this might be many months after your parent has died—you may want to begin exploring the relationship.

Begin by writing in your journal a single memory of your dead parent. It doesn't have to be a good, bad, or even major memory. For example, a woman in my group once recalled this favorite memory of her mother: "I bought her a beautiful green silk dress and she looked so pretty in it. When I remember my mother, I think of her in that dress." A man's memory of his father was also very simple and almost poetic: "Peppermint gum, tobacco, and Old Spice after-shave, with a dash of cold winter air. That was my old man."

If you choose, you can take the next step and begin to dig a little into the relationship you had with your parent. Only do this if you think you're ready! But it can be very fruitful, as you may have seen from the people in my group. In the process, not only can you learn more about yourself and your parent, but also about your relationships with all the other important people in your life.

First, in your journal, describe your parent. Then write how your parent would describe you. Describe the relationship you had with your parent. For example, did you phone or visit frequently? Did you go out together to movies, restaurants, shopping, worship services, and so on—or did you usually visit at home? Did you share hobbies or activities in common, such as playing tennis or going to the theater? How did you celebrate holidays? How were things decided between you? How were differences expressed? Did you count on your parent for advice when you had a tough decision to make?

After you have described your relationship, write down the subjects you and your parent agreed about. This can be anything at all: politics, sports, religion, morals, family traditions, and so forth. Then remember the subjects where you had the strongest disagreement. Finally, note whether or not your parent would describe things in the same way. If not, write down how you think your parent's response to these questions would be different.

Once you've finished, give it all a quick read-through, and then put it away for a couple of days. Then, read it again and add any further thoughts. Put it aside again. Wait a while before looking through it once more. This might be an exercise you can do with your siblings. Note how their perceptions differ from yours. Be ready to let their views speak for them, and yours for you. Neither is right or wrong.

Exercise 6: DRAW YOUR FAMILY SYSTEM

This is another exercise you'll want to do down the road, when you're not still feeling very sad every day. It's a way of learning more about how your family system worked—and how it has changed since the death of your parent.

Begin by describing each person in your family, including the parent who has died. After their names, list the roles they have played in your family system. For example: If you were raised by both your mother and father in what we commonly accept as the "traditional family," and were an only boy with two sisters, your role as "the boy" was clearly defined. But whether you were the first-born, middle, or youngest child will color how you were treated and what your roles and duties were. Likewise, if you were the oldest girl in a large family, you may have been given many maternal responsibilities. It may be helpful to describe a typical family meal, in as much detail as you can remember.

Then describe how the other members in your family would draw the system. Observe the differences. Why do you think your perceptions differ? (It's all the better if your partner or partners in this exercise include family members.)

Exercise 7: RECONNECT WITH SIBLING MEMORIES

One thing you'll always have in common with your siblings is your childhoods. When you were children, your roles within the family were established, and your relationships with one another were cemented. Those relationships may be causing you difficulties now, or they may be helping you better deal with your parent's loss. Remember, your siblings and you are the only ones who share certain memories.

Step back, close your eyes, and try to recall scenes from your childhood. Write down a memory or memories of something that occurred between you when you were children. Again, it can be anything that comes to mind.

One of my group members told me this recollection about a rainy Saturday afternoon: "Momma didn't usually let us out of her sight, but it had been pouring for three days, and we were home on a school vacation. I was seven and my big sister was eleven. There was a triple feature at the local movie house every Saturday, and for the first time ever, Momma let us go alone. I was so excited. Laura, my sister, was very nice to me that afternoon—for a change, I might add. She got us drinks and popcorn and we sat in the balcony. The place was packed, and even though Laura's friends were sitting a few rows ahead of us, she didn't leave me for a second to talk to them. I felt better about her after that day, and I never forgot it, even though we had plenty of arguments in the years ahead, and still do."

After you have written down a memory, say how your sibling might remember it. Compare the two. What have you discovered?

Exercise 8: ASK QUESTIONS

When a parent dies, it is common for children to begin asking questions they never asked before—or didn't have permission to ask. For example, one woman told me about the great mystery surrounding how her paternal grandfather died. She was twelve when he passed away, and nobody would talk about it. When she asked questions, they gave her vague answers that she couldn't understand. She soon learned that her grandfather's death was a taboo subject, so she stopped asking about it. Thirty years later, soon after her father's death, she became curious again, and decided to reopen the long-closed subject. Approaching her father's younger brother, her Uncle Ray, she began by asking him general information about her father's childhood on the family farm in Wisconsin. Uncle Ray responded by regaling her with the same stories she'd heard all her life. Every family has a fund of "stock memories," those remembrances which in a general way define every one of us. Athletic misadventures, childhood accidents, weddings, births, relocations, trips—they all compose the history of every family.

The woman patiently allowed Uncle Ray to spin out the family tales with an occasional question to spur him on. At what she judged to be an appropriate moment, she casually asked how her grandfather had died. At first, Uncle Ray tried to give a vague answer, but she pressed him and he finally responded with a surprisingly candid answer. It seems her grandfather had been having an affair with a young widow who lived on a nearby farm. He'd had a fatal heart attack while he was visiting her, and in the rural community, the news spread like wildfire. The ambulance that came to the woman's house was staffed by volunteers, all of whom were neighbors. The family's shame was so great that all discussion of his death was forbidden—to the confusion of this woman whose child's mind could not understand the reason for the mystery.

So, now the mystery was solved! The woman said she was glad to have a more "complete" picture of him. Her new knowledge opened up other questions and she continued to explore her family's history. She told me, "Compiling a history of the past generations of my family makes me feel less lonely. Although I am an only child and my parents are no longer living, I see I have a rich human connection to all these generations of people on both sides of the family."

Exercise 9: CREATE RITUALS

As time passes, the things you may not have been able to bear doing before can begin to bring you comfort. For example, having a certain photograph on display, listening to music that had meaning for your parent—even speaking about your parent, telling stories about him or her, or visiting the grave site. One woman compiled a memory book to show her daughter when she grew up. But really, she confided, it was for herself. In time, these "rituals" provide support instead of causing you distress.

Rituals play several roles. They help you acknowledge and mourn the loss. They symbolize what you and others in your family take with you from the person who has died. And they help you to move on in life. Many people find comfort in the rituals of religious or family tradition. But you may create your own as well.

Exercise 10: ENVISION THE FUTURE

In the last session of my group, I ask people to take some time out, find a quiet location, and try to imagine themselves five years after the death of their parent. I often hear from them later that this exercise was the most powerful in terms of restoring their hopes for the future.

These are some of the questions you might ask as you imagine yourself in five years:

• What do you look like? Are you in good physical health? Do you look different, or much the same? Are you happy, sad, full of energy, tired?

• Where are you? Do you see yourself living in a different place—maybe even a different city? Are you still living in the same place? Has anything significant changed about where you are?

• What are you doing? Do you see yourself in the same job or in a new one? Have you gone back to school? Started a business? Taken on new hobbies or volunteer activities?

• Whom are you with? Are you married? Do you have children? Is this a change from your current situation?

• Where are the other members of your family—siblings, a surviving parent, relatives—in your picture? What is your relationship with them? Has it changed?

This exercise is really a form of goal-setting. It's your way of promising yourself that you can go ahead and live a full life. Don't be surprised if there are many changes reflected in the five-year picture. The death of a parent can be a catalyst for important changes.

When an event like the death of a parent shakes your universe, you are confronted with three basic choices:

1. You can resign yourself that life is like that.
2. You can protect yourself so the trauma never happens again.
3. You can live life to the fullest.

The decision to move on and plan your future will reflect which of these choices you've made.

A YEAR LATER

More than a year has passed since the group you've come to know last met. In that period, I have worked with two more groups and watched the process of grieving and learning with them. Life's lessons continue to unfold in new and surprising ways.

This work has a great deal of meaning for me—dealing with death and its endless implications for the living. Every time I begin a new group, I feel newly humbled by the encounter and newly challenged by the question newcomers bring: "Will this group help me?"

Like all therapists, I am constantly looking for signs that the work I'm doing is really helping people. This is not a profession in which one can afford to be complacent! To be sure, there are skills involved, as well as knowledge and experience. But it is an endlessly changing craft, made so by the constant unpredictability of human experience.

In particular, these six-week sessions can be hard to evaluate. People usually come to me in the beginning stages of their grief, and leave after six weeks just beginning to explore and ask questions.

After the workshop, some people want to do more digging, sometimes in areas they hadn't anticipated. Various people keep in touch with me; they call or write to relate experiences, proudly declare positive changes, and ask advice. I am always glad to hear from them, always curious to see how they're doing. Occasionally, one of them will appear unexpectedly. This happened not too long ago. You might remember the young man I mentioned in Chapter Two who was unable to tell his loved ones how much he was hurting. Instead, he telegraphed the message to them by discarding his formerly healthy life-style and his daily exercise program. He got fat and unhealthy. "I looked like shit and I felt that way," were his words. It was the only way he knew how to cry for help.

I ran into him the other day, two years later, and I was astounded by the change. Remember, I had never known him in his fit and healthy persona. The man I saw now bore little resemblance to the one who had slumped in his chair during the group sessions. In fact, I didn't recognize him until he called out my name. He looked fit, attractive, and happy.

It's the kind of moment that therapists treasure. He told me the group helped him turn his life around, and he thanked me profusely. He said he now realized the reason he needed to look so bad, and was able to express himself in other ways.

It isn't often I get to see outcomes like that one, so directly related to discoveries made in the group.

More often, the journey is longer and the results are more oblique. But I maintain a fundamental belief in the ability of human beings to transform their lives, and over the years I have seen regular evidence that the work we do in the group does help people.

A while back, I wrote to the twelve members of the group whose journey has filled these pages. I wanted to know how they were doing and what they had discovered in the year since we met. They knew I was writing this book, and most of them were very pleased about it. They saw firsthand how hard it was to recover from a parent's death, and all agreed that this book might ease the way for others like themselves. Most of them wrote or called to let me know how they were doing, and I'd like to share some of what they told me:

Matt, whose mother's death drove him into a long period of isolation, seemed to struggle most openly during the group sessions, and was the most reluctant to do any digging about his family. At the end of six weeks, he seemed close to the place he had been when we started. I always had the impression Matt was disappointed with the group—that it was not at all what he expected. He didn't like the questions that came up or the rough-and-tumble nature of addressing real-life issues. This being the case, I was surprised when he responded immediately to my request for information with the following letter:

> For a long time after your group ended, I continued to feel empty and unattached. A huge void existed where my mother's love and friendship had been, and I didn't know where to put mine. For the first time in my life, I was not responsible to or for anyone. I was in limbo, and it was hard for me to trust anyone. I saw this pair of shoes waiting for me to fill them and move forward, but I could not bring myself to step into them. I knew

I had to do something. I often thought about the group and I'm sure you'd be surprised to hear that I've missed them. I've never been in a situation like that, and even though I convinced myself I didn't care for it, later I came to see that I liked it.

I still don't speak to my brother and I don't know if I ever will. But I've sold my mother's country house and now spend all of my time in the city. I'm trying to get it together.

Recently, my shoes took me to San Francisco for my first business trip since my mother died. I had avoided travel, but I couldn't avoid this trip. I felt lonely and miserable. There was no one to send an itinerary to, no one to call when I got there to say I'd arrived safely, no one to tell about my experiences. But here's the good news: I managed to handle a very political meeting with a skill I didn't know (or had forgotten) I had. It was like choreographing a stroll through a minefield. I did it! I feel good about it. Now I'm working on keeping those shoes filled and moving.

Thanks for putting up with me in the group. It helped me get started, and now the rest is up to me. I hope a year from now, my news is even better.

I had tears in my eyes when I finished reading Matt's letter. It reminded me of something I knew so well, but sometimes ignored: Even people who disagree a lot and seem not to be helped by the group often absorb and hear what they need to hear. I thought Matt showed great courage in being willing to continue the work on his own, even though it was so bitterly painful for him.

Irene sent me a short note, indicating that her life had picked up steam and she was doing fine. I was delighted to hear her reflections:

I've started to pay more attention to my life. I've been exercising, reading, looking at long-term goals. When my father was sick, I didn't have the energy or the time for thoughts about my future. Maybe I didn't think I had much of one. But after the group I started thinking, why not? So I've made a concerted effort to get back out in the world. My relationship with my friends has improved. My brother and I now get together on a regular basis, and this summer I went on vacation with him and his wife. He's still the same old Tom, but at least we're together more. I also visited my daughter in California in the spring, the first time I've ever flown on an airplane, if you can believe that.

I'm nearly seventy years old now, and, God willing, I still have many healthy years ahead of me. But I feel more at peace with the idea of dying. I have grown more contemplative in my life, more willing to look ahead and not be frightened.

Jane's letter was postmarked Portland, Oregon, and she wrote that she had taken a job at a hospital there.

Yes, I've moved, cats and all, to the other side of the country. I like Oregon and am enjoying my work at the hospital here. You may be thinking that it's a big change—and it is! But, Lois, I was just so unhappy it forced me to do it. So I guess good things do come from bad sometimes.

I got a lot out of your group, but I didn't do very well after it ended. I thought I had dealt with my mother's suicide, but it kept haunting me, and I started to have terrible nightmares. My priest helped me get through it, and it was he who eventually suggested I make some changes in my life. So, here I am. Since I've been out here, I've started seeing a therapist.

For a long time, I didn't think I would make it. But gradually, I've learned that I can miss my parents very much and still go on with my life in a productive way. It's a baby step, but I'm forty-three years old and I don't want to wake up at fifty, bitter and living with my cats.

I was moved by her words. Again, such evidence of strength!

Amanda also wrote, and her observations about her mother were thoughtful; they showed she had been digging. I had noticed in the group that Amanda was intensely interested in making the most of her insights. But the work she had done in the year since indicated the truth of the saying, "When you want to learn, a teacher appears." Amanda wrote:

> I have learned that I am very much my mother's daughter. For example, her independence shaped my independence, her strength increased mine, her stubbornness was matched by my own. It took her death to show me how united we were in life. Her death taught me more than anything to date that life is short no matter how long, that relationships can be both fragile and indestructable. I've learned how important it is to put our lives and concerns in perspective so we are better able to reach toward our goals and to complete our lives in satisfying and meaningful ways. There was a time I would have considered my mother to be the last person on earth who could teach me these lessons. But in her death, she has.
>
> My brother and I have recently been discussing putting my father in a group home. He's almost eighty-two now and needs more regular supervision than we're able to give. For a time, I considered bringing him to live with me. My decision not to do so might be interpreted as either selfish or a sign I'm finally choosing to live my own life.

Richard, whose father's death left him the reluctant caretaker of his "difficult" mother, had an interesting perspective on what he had been through. His observations on being a grown-up were extremely interesting. I always felt a great deal of respect for Richard. At twenty-eight, he seemed to be handling his complex responsibilities with a great deal of honesty. From the first moment I met him in my office and he admitted—to his own horror—that he wished it had been his mother who died, not his father, I knew Richard could be counted on for honesty. He wrote:

> My father's death has forced me to grow up. In some ways, I like being a grown-up, but I also find it scary. At first, I resented having to be in charge of my mother's care. When she moved into our house, I could only see it as a burden. But it hasn't been so bad. We're all adjusting. I know that taking responsibility is part of being a grown-up. It's difficult, but manageable. I have learned that it helps to find the areas you can control. So my "extended family" has instituted family meetings and we try to be clearer about what is working and how we can improve. My brother is learning quite a bit about cooperation and responsibility.
>
> Being a grown-up has also meant coming to terms with the fact that some things, like death, are inevitable and there's no rhyme or reason to it. I often wonder why death is not more a part of our everyday lives from the time we are very young. If everyone goes through this terrible grieving process, why are we so unprepared for it? I want to help my child understand the mysteries and wonder of life—including the fact that people die.

Not all the responses were filled with hope and new discoveries. Arlene sent only a brief scribbled note, saying she was now married and her life was generally going well. But she admitted:

> I still think about Daddy every day. His presence is starting to fade and that makes me feel unbearably sad. I believe it is very rare for people to have the kind of

relationship we had. It is a great gift while it is happening, but one pays the price in suffering when it ends.

What further price would Arlene pay? What price would her new husband pay? How would intimacy be possible with "Daddy" a constant, unseen presence in the room? To probe deeper, what benefit was Arlene deriving from her persistent grief and her conviction that the intimacy she shared with her father could never be achieved in any other way or with any other person? There is always a benefit, perceived or hidden, to people's behavior.

Of course, it was tempting for me to think about what I might have done differently. Until Arlene makes a commitment to look for the truth—and that may never happen—there is little that can be done. In the therapeutic professions, we call this psychological-mindedness. It is often the measure of a person's potential for success in therapy. Psychological-mindedness implies that a person is open to digging, can "use" the information presented, and can make the connection between words, thoughts, and actions. Very simply, Arlene was not psychologically minded. However, it may be that another event or series of events will get her to look at her thoughts and behavior in new ways.

People come to the group for different reasons, and not everyone benefits the same way. Some people want to retell their story and can't consider another version. They need to hold on to their one "true" version and can't let go even for a moment to see what else might be there. Those who are most upset immediately after the death are more likely to be most upset one to two years later.

But I have also learned there is no way you can predict accurately what will happen. People are full of surprises.

Patricia's letter was more encouraging. She wrote that she was continuing her investigation into her family history and it was giving her a great deal of pleasure. She also said that she was trying to figure out why she had a hard time doing less for her mother and sisters. She had this to say about herself:

> I've learned more about myself—how I handle tragedy, how I find strength, how I cope, and how intense my fears of loss are. In the process of learning to manage these anxieties and fears better, I've learned more about my family dynamics, and this has meant many important revelations. I'm trying to learn to live life to the fullest and not let my fears interfere with life's joys.

Now Patricia will have to translate her wishes to "live life to the fullest" into actions.

Mary Ann had also been on my mind a lot. Although the group sessions seemed to bring her closer to acknowledging that she and her mother had an overly dependent relationship, I could see she had a great deal of work to do in reestablishing a connection with her husband and children. But reading the letter she sent in response to my query, I saw she had gone ahead and done much of that work on her own. Mary Ann wrote:

> I can now see how my intense relationship with my mother put a strain on my marriage and made my husband feel left out. It had the same effect on my children. Now that my mother is gone and my children have moved out of the house, my husband and I have grown

much closer. We've talked about what things were like
for him in the past, and I feel that I have much to make
up to him—and to my children, too. But after the first
guilt passed, I became very optimistic about the possibilities for a new closeness. As you told us in the group,
I have many questions to ask, and I hope I'm prepared
to hear some of the answers.

I never heard from Marian, but perhaps she had found
some comfort in renewing a relationship with the neighbor
who accidentally killed her mother. This was a big chunk
of life for such a young woman; nevertheless, I like to
imagine her happily pursuing her studies and making plans
for the future. The very fact she had come to the group
and shared her experiences and emotions was an excellent
sign that she was willing to let the event help her grow,
not shrink, her heart. Nor did I hear from Helen, but I
hoped she was doing well.

Some time after I wrote to the group, I received an
apologetic phone call from Barry. He had never gotten
around to writing, he said, but proceded to tell me on the
phone about the various changes in his life.

Yes, he had told his family he was gay, and they had
taken it pretty well. He was less certain of how it would
be when he brought his new partner home for the holidays,
but he sounded quite cheerful about it, so I guessed he was
ready. Barry told me that for him the group was an en-
lightening experience that got him moving on all the un-
finished business of his life. As part of that process, he was
seeing a therapist.

A phone call from Eileen was more disturbing. I could
immediately hear the familiar anger in her voice. She said
she had put my letter aside and forgotten about it, but had

woken out of a sound sleep the night before, remembering that she had to call me.

She told me her news was not very good, and when I asked her to explain what she meant by that, she rambled into a tirade about her brother and how many problems she was having with him.

She ended with the "big news" that she and her husband were getting a divorce. "So, I guess I won't have to worry about having a baby now."

People tend to repeat patterns, trying to find some resolution to an old problem. I could hear in Eileen's voice how much energy was being gobbled up by her anger.

I do this work because I believe in people's ability to change, fundamentally and truly. Who can say how people will learn and whom they'll choose to teach them? It's a mystery that is not always revealed. It's as though they are on a road and come to a place where a large tree has fallen across their path. They can't go around it, over it, or under it. Yet they know somehow the road has to be cleared so they can keep moving. It might require only a shovel. Or maybe a forklift. Or sometimes a huge tractor truck.

Since our meetings recreate the feelings of family, it is not surprising that the very things that get in people's way on the outside also do here. But it is always my belief that once a question or idea gets planted, it has a chance to grow—no matter how infertile the soil.

I believe that every human being wants to be happy; it is as fundamental as breathing. Sometimes people choose to let life give momentum to their quest; others shirk life and view it as a threat. In both cases, the goal of happiness is the same, but the path taken and the outcome are different. Fortunately, there's always a new chance to start off on another path. There is always hope.

READING LIST

Angel, Marc D. *The Orphaned Adult: Confronting the Death of a Parent*. New York: Insight Books, Human Service Press, 1987.

Brooks, Anne M. *The Grieving Time: A Year's Account of Recovering from Loss*. New York: Harmony Books, 1985.

Colgrove, Melba, Harold Bloomfield, and Peter McWilliams. *How to Survive the Loss of a Love*. New York: Bantam, 1976.

Donnelly, Katherine Fair. *Recovering from the Loss of a Parent*. New York: Dodd, Mead, 1987.

Furman, Erna. *A Child's Parent Dies: Studies in Childhood Bereavement*. New Haven, London: Yale University Press, 1974.

Grollman, Earl A. *Time Remembered: A Journal for Survivors*. Boston: Beacon Press, 1987.

———, ed. *Explaining Death to Children*. Boston: Beacon Press, 1967.

James, John W., and Frank Cherry. *The Grief Recovery Handbook*. New York: Harper & Row, 1988.

Kubler-Ross, Elisabeth. *On Death and Dying.* New York: Macmillan, 1969.

———. *Death, the Final Stage of Growth.* Englewood Cliffs, N.J.: Prentice Hall, 1975.

Kushner, Harold S. *When Bad Things Happen to Good People.* New York: Schocken Books, 1981.

Lerner, Harriet Goldhor, Ph.D. *The Dance of Anger.* New York: Harper & Row, 1987.

Lightner, Candy. *Giving Sorrow Words—How to Cope with Grief and Get On with Your Life.* New York: Warner Books, 1990.

McGoldrick, Monica; *Living Beyond Loss: Death in the Family,* ed. Randy Gerson. New York: W. W. Norton, 1991.

Myers, Edward. *When Parents Die: A Guide for Adults.* New York: Viking, 1986.

Piper, William E., Mary McCallum, and F. A. Hassan Azim. *Adaptation to Loss Through Short-term Group Psychotherapy.* New York: The Guilford Press, 1992.

Rollins, Betty. *Last Wish.* New York: Simon and Schuster, 1985.

Staudacher, Carol. *Men and Grief.* New York: New Harbinger Publications, 1991.

Stiles, Norman. *I'll Miss You, Mr. Hooper.* New York: Random House and Children's Television Workshop, 1984.

Tannen, Deborah, Ph.D. *You Just Don't Understand: Women and Men in Conversation.* New York: William Morrow and Company, 1990.

Vail, Elaine. *A Personal Guide to Living with Loss.* New York: John Wiley and Sons, 1982.

Viorst, Judith. *Necessary Losses.* New York: Simon and Schuster, 1986.

———. *The 10th Good Thing About Barney.* New York: Atheneum, 1971.